Of the Trees and the Birds

Ian Parsons

Whittles Publishing

Whittles Publishing Ltd,
Dunbeath,
Caithness, KW6 6EG,
Scotland, UK
www.whittlespublishing.com

ISBN 978-184995-574-4

Printed and bound in Great Britain by
TJ Books Limited, Padstow, Cornwall

Contents

Prologue

I am in a large field of lush grass, a typical mid-Devon field in which the typical black-and-white dairy cows can often be found. I am standing still, looking in admiration at what is in front of me. I am not cow-watching, though; I am tree-watching. In front of me, incongruously placed in the centre of this expanse of lush pasture, is an oak tree, a majestic example of one of our two native species of the large oak genus. It is huge, it is beautiful, a brilliantly picturesque example of an old open-grown oak tree. Several heavy limbs fan out from around the rugged trunk, arcing upwards and creating a perfect dendrite form against the blue sky beyond. This is a tree that has grown up alone. It hasn't had to compete with other trees for light, and it hasn't had its branches constricted by the growth of neighbouring trees; this is a tree that has had the freedom to grow as it *wanted* to grow. The result is magnificent. What a tree!

I walk up to the trunk, whose bulk completely dwarfs me. The vertical ridges and their corresponding crevices running up the bark give it the well-worn appearance of an experienced campaigner, and it has the patina that only old trees can have. I reach out and touch it, running my fingers over the hard unyielding ridges and deep into the furrows. I take a step back from the vastness of the trunk and get my extra-long tape out of my pocket. This isn't going to be easy. The trunk is far too vast for me to put my arms around, and there is no way I can hold the end of the measuring tape in one hand and toss it around the trunk to the other; this should be a two-person measuring job. But I am here on my own; it's just me and the tape. I force the metal end of my tape into a furrow in the bark, trying to jam it in between the ridges, eventually getting it wedged, then I start to walk around the trunk, unwinding the tape as I go, only to find that the end of the tape drops from its hold and falls to the grass below.

Eventually, on the fourth or fifth attempt, and after much muttering on my part, I manage to wedge it in sufficiently well for it to stay there, and off I set around the tree again, stumbling over the uneven ground, pushed up and broken by the massive roots lying beneath. It turns out that the tree's circumference is roughly 5½ metres, a good size, and a quick bit of mental arithmetic later I have a very rough figure for its age; somewhere around the 220 mark.[1]

This is a tree, then, that pullulated forth from its acorn when King George III was still on the throne, Napoleon was the new *de facto* leader of the fledgling French republic, and Ludwig van Beethoven was premiering his Symphony No. 1 in Austria.

I step backwards, away from the trunk, and look up into the spreading branches. 'What are you doing, growing here?' I ask the tree. But it stays mute. This tree may be over 200 years old, but it isn't a remnant of an old land use for this area; this oak hasn't grown up in a woodland only to find itself an arboreal island after its neighbours have been felled and removed. This particular tree has always grown in this type of open landscape, and given the county's long history of pastoral farming it's likely that it has spent its entire life growing in what can only be described as a farm field. I can tell all of this by reading the tree. The form of a mature tree tells you much about its history, and this oak's large open crown, supported by the massive limbs that radiate out from the trunk in all directions, state very clearly that this tree has always grown in an open expanse and that it is not a survivor from a more arboreous landscape.

There can only be one explanation for why this beautiful tree is here, growing as it is in this open landscape, and that is that it was planted here, planted in the open ground of a field. But as I lose myself gazing into the maze of leafy branches above me, I don't think it was planted by a human; instead I think this tree, this magnificent specimen of a pedunculate oak, was planted by a bird, in a classic example of the relationships of the trees and the birds.

Oak Bark

---

1 Ageing trees in this manner is fraught with error, but short of reading the rings within, it is the only practicable method when out in the field. I have followed the formula described by Alan Mitchell in his *Trees of Britain*, a book described in the Acknowledgements.

Introduction

In the world of natural history, amidst the sheer wonder of all it contains, are two of my favourite things, trees and birds. I am not alone in this; birdwatching in Britain is huge, be it people travelling miles to see a rarity, or people who don't even think themselves as birders taking great pleasure from the sparrows in the park eating breadcrumbs around the benches. Birds are incredibly popular. And so are trees.

Trees might not have the same passionate following that birds have – people don't tend to drive miles to see a rare one (although I have) – but trees can certainly generate a lot of passion in people, especially when we feel that 'our' tree or trees are under threat.[2] I have always loved trees, even before I realised that I was indeed a dendrophile. The playground of my infant school in the late 1970s had a collection of prostrate logs, giants of potential fun to the little me, and my school friends and I used our imagination to turn them into all sorts of wonderful things. I loved those logs, loved how they felt as I grappled with them during the break times. Each one of them was different, with varying curves and bumps and textures, all of which aided our childhood creativity as we clambered all over them, occasionally slipping off onto the unforgiving non-safety surface of playground concrete below. They may just have been dead trees sat on concrete, but I loved them nonetheless.

But then my primary school lacked playground logs; its surface was instead decorated with bright paint, delineating pitches to play football on and creating numbered boxes for the use of those that preferred hopscotch to kicking a ball around. In comparison to my infant school, the play at primary school was structured and laid out, no room for a creative imagination and a big log. But outside the school, growing opposite its entrance in the middle of a tightly mown grass green, was a large horse chestnut. If ever there was a tree for a young boy to love it was a horse chestnut, the source of that autumnal playtime favourite and playground currency, the conker. But actually, it wasn't those beautiful brown seeds that initially captured my imagination – it was the tree's large springtime sticky buds. I'm not

---

2 The passion that people feel for trees can quickly turn to outrage, with the reaction to the felling of the Sycamore Gap tree in autumn 2023 being a good example. Trees can mean many things to people; they can become part of our lives.

sure of the exact details – it was a long time ago now – but I do remember a teacher giving us each a small shoot from a horse chestnut, a knobbly twig topped off with a large fat sticky bud. Our task was, I think, to take it home over the Easter holidays and draw it each day as its leaves burst out of that bud.

I was fascinated by this event, initially intrigued that an apparently dead twig could still produce a leaf, and then enthralled as it went on to do so, throwing out its multi-fingered leaf before finally running out of resources. I was probably seven, or maybe eight, when I took this sticky-budded twig home with me; however old I was, the experience of doing so has always stayed with me, so much so that I recently did it again. Forty years may have passed, but earlier this year, having snapped off a twig on one of our walks before carefully placing it in a vase of water on the kitchen window sill, I still delighted in watching the brown bud burst forth into a bright green leaf.

As a youngster, lacking in the adult inhibition of self-preservation, I soon discovered that trees were also great to climb, a three-dimensional world just ripe for youthful exploration. My first memories of those trees are of course heavily skewed by my small childhood frame; I particularly remember two growing together on a bank on a large area of common land that lay to the north and east of the town where I grew up. Between them they had produced an intertwined tangled mass of sprawling branches that offered seemingly unlimited pathways through them. I can also remember the surprise – and, yes, disappointment – at returning to these trees as a young adult and discovering they were actually very low-growing examples of Portuguese laurel, giving me a sudden revelation that my childhood adventures in the treetops were not quite as daring as I had believed. I was no Baron Cosimo[3] after all.

Walking to big school, a name that is apt for what was the largest comprehensive in England at the time, took me either along tree-lined roads or a scrubbed and treed-up and semi-wild disused railway cutting. The school itself was so large that it sprawled over two sites, separated by a public park replete with dozens of large trees. Whether I was going to school, going from lesson to lesson or returning home again at the end of the day, I was constantly passing trees. It was around this time that the seed of becoming a ranger germinated in my head, I took more interest in the trees that I saw. Identifying the whitebeams that grew along the roads I walked through is a memory that stays with me, as does the memory of definitely not telling my mates that I knew what trees they were, for fear of mickey-taking.

I'm not sure when birds first flew into my consciousness. I've still got the *Ladybird Book of Garden Birds*, but as this was published six years before I was born it doesn't help me date when I started to take notice of birds. I have many memories of looking out of my bedroom window and watching gulls flying in loose formation across the sky, I have a memory of watching a blackbird tugging hard on a worm in our lawn and I can also remember a semi-tame jackdaw that appeared one day and perched on my and my sister's shoulders – the

---

3 A character in the wonderful book *The Baron in the Trees* by Italo Calvino, first published in 1957.

hilarity of which was cut short when it started to painfully, but playfully I'm sure, nip our ear lobes.

I can clearly remember a walk with my dad when I was probably around 11 years of age and seeing a bird I just didn't know. I can remember going home and looking it up in a book, flicking through the limited pages and coming up with great grey shrike. Now that was exciting, but I still also remember the disappointment of my dad telling me it looked nothing like that. And he was right. It was a northern wheatear, a bird that I now know as being absolutely amazing, but for a long time afterwards it was a bird that just wasn't as exciting as something that had the alternative name of butcher bird.

Northern wheatears aren't birds we associate with trees, and there are many species of birds that don't use trees at all,[4] but almost invariably when we humans think of trees we think of the birds within them. They go together, and they have done for a very long time. The birds and the trees have been together for not just millennia but mega-annums, millions and millions of years, a period of time so long that we struggle to comprehend it. In contrast, we humans, *Homo sapiens*, evolved only around 300,000 years ago – no more than a mere snip in geological time. Because trees and birds have been around together for so long it should be no surprise to find that they have formed relationships. Some are very basic – for example birds using trees as launch pads to get airborne – but some have obviously evolved, a good example being how trees provide enticements for birds to spread their seeds. Some of these evolved relationships are simple, whilst others are much more complicated and involved. One thing for certain is that there are many relationships between birds and trees that we still haven't noticed. Relationships between species – be they close relatives or from completely different kingdoms, as trees and birds are –are an everyday feature of life on our planet. It is how nature functions, how life works, but it is all too easy to miss these relationships, and even with the ones we do notice, it is also very easy to underestimate just how complex they are. Sadly, it is also far too easy for us to throw proverbial spanners in their works.

I love losing myself in nature, and I strongly believe that it is an important thing for us to do. I have no doubt that it's very good for our mental health and general wellbeing to just sit and watch wildlife functioning around us, disconnecting ourselves from our disconnected world, and reconnecting with a world that is fully connected. Whether I am in the midst of the countryside or sitting in the back bedroom looking out over the garden, watching wildlife and what it's doing is always a fascination for me. Whilst it's good to switch off and let your brain wander, it's also good to let your brain wonder at what you are watching. 'Why?' is a question I love to ask people and to ask myself: Why is that oak tree growing in the middle of that field? or Why is that blackbird feeding in *that* blackthorn bush and not in the others next to it? Trying to interpret the behaviour you see when watching wildlife

---

4 There are even some that have never ever seen a tree. What an emperor penguin would make of one is anybody's guess!

is, at least for me, one of its big attractions in the first place. By watching and questioning, you enter a world that might not be immediately obvious, but it is definitely a world that we should try and discover; it is the world of ecological relationships, a world of symbiosis. It is a world I love.

This is not a scientific book, nor is it a careful analysis of data to prove or disprove. It is my take on the relationships that I know about, or at least I think I know about. As I researched this book I read lots of great scientific papers, but it is my interpretation of them that you are reading now, and any mistakes within this book are entirely my own. I hope that this book will encourage you to look at what you see with a more enquiring eye. The relationships between the trees and the birds are varied, brilliant and in many cases mind-blowing. We still don't know everything about this world – I suspect that we will never fully know everything about it – but one thing that is for certain is that this is a world well worth exploring. I find it fascinating, and I hope you will too.

To get to grips with it, though, we need to first of all look at the origins of the two main players: the trees and the birds.

Part One
Origins

Origins

A brief history of trees

As well as asking Why? a lot, there is one other question which I always like to ask people – a question that appears at first to be incredibly simple, but is in fact very difficult to answer. That question is 'What is a tree?' We might like to think we know what a tree is – after all, we see them around us all the time and we all recognise them for what they are – but what are they, actually? What *is* it that makes a tree a tree?

Ask a child to draw a tree and they will almost invariably draw the classic lollipop tree, a central stick with a round canopy at its top. As childish as that may be, that is pretty much what most people think a tree is: a long single trunk with branches and leaves at the top. The problem is that not all trees are like that. They don't follow our rules, they don't conform to our ideas of what they should look like; many of them naturally have more than one stem, or trunk, and whilst many of them are often tall, there are also plenty that are not. Most of us can recognise a silver birch, a beautiful and common tree that is native to the UK; the attractive white bark of the species makes it a favourite arboreal choice for planting in gardens and amenity areas, creating beacons of white in seas of green. They are relatively tall and conform to the classic tree image, with their single stem easily reaching 25 metres or more in height. We can surely say, therefore, that birches are trees.

But what about the dwarf birch? This is a very close relative of the silver birch and is also a native of the UK. Native it may be, but this tree of the Arctic north is nowhere near as familiar to us as its silvery relative; this is a tundra tree that is at its very southern limit in the UK, and restricted to only our highest mountain areas. Sadly, its continuation as a tree of the British Isles is threatened by climate change, and it has already undergone a severe decline in range here as our rapidly warming climate is forcing it higher up the mountains on which it is found. It can't cope with the rising temperatures at the altitudes it once thrived at, so its distribution in Britain is pushed higher and higher. But our mountains are of a finite height, so this tree's future in our country is at risk …

Prostrate juniper

… but back to the point. The dwarf birch, as its name strongly suggests, isn't a tree that conforms to the classic tree image. Its tallest examples may reach the rather undizzying heights of a metre or so, but most of them are prostrate, multi-stemmed ground-huggers, similar in appearance to the prostrate juniper in the photo. Yet the dwarf birch *is* a birch, and birches are trees.

Well, if it isn't height that's the key factor in making a tree a tree, perhaps it's woody stems that define them. After all, trees have woody stems, don't they? Except … palm trees don't, nor do banana trees. Meanwhile gorse and heather have woody stems, but they're not trees.[5]

So it can rapidly get confusing when trying to define exactly what a tree is.

Quite simply, the only feature that makes a tree a tree is that it's what we humans have decided to call a vastly disparate group of plants. There is no proper definition of a tree, no biological exposition. They don't belong in a single taxonomic group like birds; trees are, if you like, a purely human concept. They are found throughout the entire plant kingdom. There is no tree family to which they belong, and many of the trees you have growing in your garden, the ones you see in the local park, and the ones planted in your local supermarket

5 Except one species of heather which is called a tree; the tree heather (*Erica arborea*) which is found throughout the Mediterranean basin and can reach heights of 7 metres, completely dwarfing the very closely related species of heather we have in Britain, species we would never consider as trees.

car park are completely unrelated to one another. The common hawthorn is more closely related to the tiny and delicate wild strawberry than it is to the beech tree, and the so-called English oak is as closely related to the so-called Scots pine as we are to a haddock.

Trees are a perfect example of something called convergent evolution, in which unrelated species evolve similar features to fill certain ecological niches. The classic dendrite form of a tree has evolved many times over during the long history of our planet, with the first 'trees' appearing in the fossil record some 385 million years ago in the form of the *Wattieza*, a treefern-like plant that could attain heights of around 8 metres. At that time other plants also evolved the dendrite way of life, the lycophytes – a lineage of plants that still survives today – forming a wide range of simple but tall 'trees' that formed the extensive forests of the Carboniferous period from around 360 million years ago. The lycophytes that survive today, though, are not trees, nor could we imagine calling them such; they are club mosses and quillworts, plants that attain heights of centimetres rather than metres – but back in the day, lycophyte species like the lepidodendron would have been recognisable to us as trees, reaching towering heights of 40 or 50 metres, and with stems over a metre across at the base. It is the fossilised remains of these early trees, and the other plants they shared the Carboniferous forests with, that we would later exploit millions of years later as coal. Hence the term 'fossil fuel'.

Those early trees reproduced by spores, but a revolution in reproduction soon arrived. Spores would be kept by some, but a new wave of species was coming and they would reproduce by seed. Known as the gymnosperms, these new kids on the block arrived in the fossil record around 300 million years ago, and these seed-producing plants flourished, soon dominating the plant kingdom, evolving into a vast group of species within which we find conifers and ginkgoes, trees that are very much still with us. Conifers were particularly prevalent, evolving into a wide variety of families and species, but today only a small percentage of this type of tree survive. Mind you, that's still over 600 species, but they are remnants of a once vast number of cone-bearing species. The ginkgoes, which were also once incredibly diverse and numerous, although not on the scale of the conifers, would virtually die out during the Cretaceous period. which began 150 million years ago, leaving us with just one species, the ginkgo, which has hardly changed in all those millions of years. The ginkgo is now extremely rare, restricted to perhaps just one truly wild population; however it can be found across the world due to its long history of cultivation and its popularity as an amenity and garden species. The pedant in me has to point out that the tree's name is actually wrong, a result of a misspelling 300 years ago during a translation; the tree's real name in our westernised alphabet should be ginkjo.[6]

Some of the conifer species that have survived and are still with us include the Araucarias, trees that probably first evolved around 120 million years ago. One of the most familiar

---

6 It was German naturalist Engelbert Kaempfer that made the mistake; it was then copied by the father of modern taxonomy, Carl Linnaeus, in his writings and so the mistake became the name.

of these trees is a South American native that has been a popular tree in Britain since it was introduced in the year 1792. It is the Chilean pine, a tree that isn't a pine at all; but for most of us this is irrelevant, as we much prefer to call it the monkey puzzle. These spectacular trees can now be found throughout much of Britain, their distinctive form noticeable in public parks, large gardens, even small gardens, where they soon dominate, and often on the driveways and in the landscaped gardens of stately homes. Trees can be subject to the whims of fashion, much like everything else, and in the late Georgian and early Victorian eras if you wanted to flaunt your status to your friends and business partners it became *de rigueur* to have at least one of these trees growing in your grounds.

It was in this sort of setting that the tall spiky tree obtained the colloquial name that we all know it by today. A baronet was busy showing his guests his grounds and no doubt took great pleasure in pointing out a specimen of this strange-looking, and highly fashionable, tree. One of his gentlemen guests nonchalantly remarked: 'It would puzzle a monkey to climb that.' A throwaway comment perhaps, but one that has for some reason stuck. It was a remark referring to its incredible spiky scale-like leaves,

Monkey puzzle

growing as they do out of the trunk as well as all along the branches, and whilst these might indeed be irksome to any monkeys trying to climb it, the tree evolved long before monkeys did. Those sharp leaves weren't there to protect the tree from our arboreal ancestors, they were most likely there to protect it from the browsing of sauropods such as the brontosaurus.

As the Cretaceous period dawned around 145 million years ago, a new form of plant arrived in the fossil record, the result of yet another revolution in reproduction. These new plants were the angiosperms or, as we tend to call them, the flowering plants. These new examples of plant life would go on to evolve into the majority of plants that we know today, including the broadleaf trees that we are so familiar with. It is likely that the angiosperms evolved from one of the gymnosperms, but currently the origins of the flowering plants remain a mystery lost in the depths of time. One of the earliest examples of an angiosperm to turn up in the fossil record were the magnolias, those showy trees so popular in suburban gardens. These were swiftly followed by many more, including the first members of the family that today comprises such well-known trees as the oaks and the common beech, a family with a fossil record dating back to 100 million years ago.

Monkey puzzle close-up

The tree, in one form or another, has been around for a long time, far longer than we can really comprehend; to cover their history fully is a whole book in itself. It still amazes me that some of the trees that we can see today are so old in their lineage that they shared the Earth with the dinosaurs. But then it shouldn't amaze me really, because they still do.

A brief history of birds

Birds go back a very long time. Perhaps not as long as the trees, but nonetheless they have been inhabitants of this planet far longer than we have. The easiest way to demonstrate exactly how long birds have been on Earth is by stating the fact that birds – all birds, be they ostriches or hummingbirds – are dinosaurs.

Richard Owen's 'terrible lizards' still exist.[7] As I write this now, one of them is flitting about the garden outside my window, and whilst a blackbird might not look a lot like a Tyrannosaurus Rex, it is still a dinosaur. The birds are the only surviving lineage of the once globally dominant dinosaurs, and whilst a meteorite put paid to the rest of their kind around 66 million years ago, in an occurrence snappily named the Cretaceous–Paleogene Extinction Event, the birds somehow survived, slipping through that evolutionary eye of a needle and flourishing on this side of it.

Blackbird

---

7 It was the Victorian biologist Richard Owen who coined the name 'dinosaur', which means 'terrible reptile'.

Robin

Watching nature documentaries as a child, I was often informed that large reptiles such as the saltwater crocodile and the equally fearsome alligator of America's swamplands were direct links to the mighty dinosaurs. This was highly believable stuff for an 11-year-old, let's face it; it doesn't take much of a leap in a child's imagination to marry up an image of a large saltwater croc with that of a T-Rex or similar; dinosaurs were ferocious-looking lizards, and crocodiles were also ferocious-looking lizards. Simple.

But these mighty reptiles are not descendants of the dinosaurs; in fact they pre-date them. The *crocodilia* are older than Owen's terrible lizards, their lineage evolving long before that of the dinosaurs, and whilst I was avidly lapping up what I was being told on those television documentaries, the true descendants of the dinosaurs were actually out in the garden, serenading the evening sun as the day drew to its conclusion. The trouble is, especially to an excitable 11-year-old, a robin doesn't exactly fit our traditional view of what a dinosaur should look like.

It is only relatively recently that the assertion that birds are in fact dinosaurs has become accepted. In the 1970s and the 1980s scientists started to say with increasing confidence that birds were *descended* from dinosaurs. But this was in fact nothing new; the great Victorian biologist T.H. Huxley had concluded this 100 years earlier – but 'descending from' is not the same as 'being', and there was a big gap in the knowledge of how exactly scaly-skinned dinosaurs had evolved into feathered birds. All that changed in the 1990s with some remarkable fossil discoveries in China.

One of the distinguishing features of a bird is that it has feathers. Nothing else that we know of has these wonderful structures, so basically if it has feathers it's a bird. That's a very simple rendering of a biological rule, but it is – or at least was – true. Feathers means bird. The problem with this rule is that the fossils in China revealed something incredible; dinosaurs had feathers too. The fossils in question were of small theropods called maniraptors, dinosaurs that ran on their rear legs, pursuing their prey.

One of the superstars of the dinosaur world, thanks to Hollywood, is the velociraptor, a type of maniraptor made famous by the 1990s blockbuster film *Jurassic Park*. The film version of the velociraptor and the real version were similar in that they were both fast-running predators, but that's pretty much where the similarity ends. In reality, velociraptors were smaller than their big screen counterparts (everything is bigger in Hollywood!); they were only 1–2 metres in length. But they were feisty creatures nonetheless, one of the most famous dinosaur fossils of all, known as the Fighting Dinosaurs, shows a velociraptor locked in mortal combat with a heavily armoured protoceratops. But the biggest difference between the film version and reality is that Hollywood portrayed the dinosaur in the traditional manner, with the classic scaly reptilian skin, but as the fossils from China (and subsequent later discoveries) showed, the velociraptors were feathered. This had profound implications. After all, if one of the defining characteristics of a bird is that it has feathers, then these dinosaurs with feathers were, according to the rules, actually birds.

Sometimes in life it is a good idea to step away from something and look at it in a different way, and when this sound advice was followed with these feathered fossils it was soon realised that actually, instead of the dinosaurs being birds, the birds were, and still are, dinosaurs. The birds that we all know and take for granted today – the birds that bring us so much pleasure and generate so much interest, the birds that are outside your window right now – are a type of maniraptor (as were the legendary T-Rex and the velociraptors), a branch of the theropod dinosaurs. It turns out that dinosaurs are not extinct at all. They are all around us.

To help smooth over the rather inconvenient fact that dinosaurs aren't as extinct as we once thought, the terms 'non-avian dinosaurs' and 'avian dinosaurs' have been created. The avian dinosaur lineage has continued to this day, whilst the non-avian lineage died out in the aftermath of that meteorite strike all those millions of years ago. Many species of dinosaur are indeed extinct, but not all of them.

Fossils of a very bird-like creature, the archaeopteryx, are among some of the best-known of them all. When it was discovered, there were many who proposed that this species (or as it actually turned out, group of species) was the missing link between the ground-dwelling dinosaurs and the birds. The fossils show many features common to both; the wings had what are clearly flight feathers, but it also had small teeth (something birds do not have[8]) and a long reptile-like bony tail (again, something lacking in birds). However, it has now been concluded that instead of being a direct ancestor of the creatures that we call birds today, the archaeopteryx was a close relative of it – a cousin, if you like – an offshoot in the evolution of birds that ultimately, and unfortunately for the archaeopteryx, led nowhere. There are many more evolutionary dead ends than there are successful lineages, and the archaeopteryx was one of these cul de sacs of life. Although, of course, it did eventually produce stunning fossils.

Archaeopteryx were large corvid-sized creatures, somewhere between a crow and a raven, and, based on their feathers and wing structure, they could indeed fly. How they flew, though, is open to debate. Lots and lots of debate. Over the years there have been many scientific papers published about the flight of this ancient animal, some research suggesting it was only capable of gliding, but others saying it was capable of powered flight – i.e. it flapped its wings to generate lift as modern flying birds do today – and yet others suggest that whilst it was capable of powered flight, its flight was of a type that differs from that of modern birds. Then there is the research that states that whilst archaeopteryx were primarily gliders they were also capable of bursts of wing movement that would sustain the creatures' flight for longer than gliding alone. Basically, over the years every form of flight has been proposed for this long-dead evolutionary dead end.

But there's not just debate on how they flew; there is also debate about how archaeopteryx actually got into the air in the first place – something it would obviously need to do before

---

8 The reason behind the saying 'as rare as hen's teeth'!

it actually flew in whatever manner it used to travel through the skies. Did it run across the open ground in the manner of the velociraptors, gathering speed before opening its wings to catch the air, enabling it to get some lift and to glide? Or did it scramble up vegetation or rocks and then launch itself off them, opening its wings out as it fell? The truth is nobody actually knows; all we can do is make guesses, albeit educated guesses, at how this animal got into the air and then, once there, how it actually moved through it.

One of the intriguing features that the archaeopteryx had were claws on their wings. These claws, you won't be surprised to learn, have also been the subject of much debate. We don't think of modern birds generally having claws on their wings, which are, of course, forelimbs equivalent to our arms – but some species of birds do, especially the ducks and swans, and if you have ever handled live chickens you will know that these too have a claw as part of their wing. In most cases these claws are vestigial, remnants of a past usage that evolution has now made redundant. But there is one bird that is famous for having functional claws on its wings, and that's the hoatzin of South America.

The hoatzin is an unusual bird that inhabits the wet forest areas and mangroves of the Amazon basin and surrounding country. With its bare blue face and spiky crest, coupled with its long neck, long tail and proportionally large feet, it is distinctive in looks as well as biology. There is only the one species of hoatzin. It is truly a unique bird, and where it sits in the family tree of modern birds has long been a puzzle; at various times it has been placed with the grouse, the rails, the bustards, the sandgrouse, the pigeons and even the cuckoos. However, modern genetic studies have now revealed that it doesn't belong in any of these groups; the hoatzin is the sole remaining species of a line of birds that branched off from the evolutionary tree of modern birds around 64 million years ago, just after that famous meteorite hit. There are no relations left. This is a bird that doesn't have much of a Christmas card list.

Hoatzins are herbivores, mainly eating the leaves of the trees in which they live. Leaves are not the easiest of things to digest, especially for birds, and to cope with this foliage-based diet the hoatzin has evolved a unique digestive system not unlike that of a mammalian ruminant, using bacteria to ferment the leaves before digesting them. Unlike mammals, though, these birds don't have a rumen, but their digestive system is highly modified with several chambers to aid the process, including a greatly enlarged crop in which the fermentation takes place. But all this specialisation has, in turn, affected the bird's flight capability; the wing muscles used for flight and the sternum that they are attached to have had to play second fiddle to this unique digestive system in the finite space of the bird's body, and as a result the bird is a relatively poor flyer. The highly specialised digestive system might compromise the bird's flight capabilities, but it does also confer on it some form of protection from our own predatory activities. As a result of the fermentation processes in its digestive tract and the various chemical compounds contained in the leaves that the bird eats, it could be politely said that the bird has a certain odour about it. Hoatzins stink. The smell is said to be so strong that humans very rarely hunt it for food even though it is relatively large and easy to catch, believing that the smell of the bird will also be reflected in the taste of it.

Adult hoatzins don't possess claws in their wing structure, but the young birds do, and those claws are anything but vestigial. The bird's nests are invariably built over water, and the young move about in their arboreal world long before they can fly, scrambling through the maze of branches using their large feet and their wing claws to grip the branches. When a predator threatens, the flightless youngsters opt for the somewhat drastic overboard option, letting go of the branches and tumbling down through them into the water below, where they are then able to swim under water. Once the danger has passed, these young birds haul themselves out of the water and back up through the branches of the trees, using their claws as climbing aids.

The strange appearance of the hoatzin, coupled with its poor flight and the claws on the wings, led to comparisons with the fossilised remains of archaeopteryx. Was this South American bird a descendant of that famous fossil? Is the hoatzin a prototype bird? Modern thought now believes not. It appears that hoatzins evolved long after the archaeopteryx had reached the end of its cul de sac; the hoatzin is an old bird, but still a relatively modern one. However, the manner in which those young hoatzins clamber back up into the branches after their plummet from peril makes me wonder how the actual ancestors of modern birds first used trees. It is no great leap, surely, to suggest that millions and millions of years ago they did something very similar in what could have been the first interaction between birds and trees: a primitive bird using its wing claws and large reptilian feet to clamber up the trunk and branches of a primitive tree, perhaps to escape a ground-based predator. We just don't know. But if that is what it did, if that is why the first 'bird' went up a tree, it inadvertently started an enduring relationship between the avian and the arboreal worlds. Because by gaining the height required to avoid being eaten it would also, crucially, have gained the height that would have enabled it to launch itself into the air, enabling it to glide away on open wings or even to power away on some sort of flapping wings. We will never know what actually happened, nor will we know when it happened, but it must have happened in some form, and from that moment, lost forever in time, the enduring relationship between trees and birds was born.

The avian dinosaurs we share the planet with today are biologically classed as belonging to the modern birds: neornithes. It is believed that these first evolved around 100 million years ago. This group of modern birds would have then undertaken a varied and rapid diversification of form around the time of the meteorite mass extinction that led to the demise of the non-avian dinosaurs. It was these neornithes that evolved into the families and species we know today. Birds and trees have been interacting for a very long time indeed.

Relationships

We need to talk about relationships, or at least have a brief discussion about them. The world wide web is nothing new – it's just a term that we've borrowed. Everything in the natural world is connected, and those connections are many and varied; it is *this* that's the true world wide web – and it doesn't need hard drives, software or electricity to function. There is nothing in nature that exists in isolation, in its own one lucky prize; if it did, it couldn't survive.

'Symbiosis' is the catch-all word used to describe the relationships that exist between living things on Earth, but the word started off from more humble beginnings; it was first used in the world of lichen, and its use began with the then shocking discovery that what were thought to be very simple plants were actually anything but.

Lichens aren't plants at all. They are a combination of two very separate things: algae and fungi. When we casually look at lichens forming circular shapes on gravestones and the like they may seem like very simple life forms – but they are not. The lichens you see on a tree's bark, or on a rock's surface, or on a gravestone are perfect examples of a complex mutually beneficial relationship between species from two different kingdoms.[9] The fungi benefit from the algae's ability to photosynthesise (one of the few things that the amazing fungal world cannot do itself) and produce carbohydrates that the fungi can then feed on, whilst the fungi benefit the fragile algae by safeguarding them, holding them in place and protecting them from an environment otherwise too harsh for them to survive in alone. Another more succinct way of looking at lichens has been expressed by the biologist Trevor Goward of the University of British Columbia, who came up with the epigram: 'Lichens are fungi that have discovered agriculture'.

Lichens are controversial and confusing; they make us question what is actually a species, what is an individual being? Lichens are the anarchists of the living world, ripping up the rule book (but only a rule book that we humans have written) and destroying the neat order of life we so painstakingly tried to construct. It was only in 1867 that a Swiss botanist, Simon Schwendener, discovered that lichens were actually this combination of algae and fungi, a mixture of living things coming together to form another living thing. He wrote up his discovery and on publishing it immediately caused controversy, many other prominent biologists and self-proclaimed lichenologists ridiculing the very suggestion that lichens were a combination. In their eyes it just couldn't be true, as it was a theory that went against the very bedrock of human biological thought – a bedrock of belief that stated unequivocally that every living thing was autonomous in its existence. Schwendener's proclamation was so controversial that even the creator of Peter Rabbit weighed in.

Beatrix Potter is today best known as a children's author whose literary work and

---

9 In this context 'kingdom' is a biological term used in the fundamental classification of all living things. We think of the animal kingdom and the plant kingdom, but there are several more, although exactly how many and whether the term is still relevant is yet another hotly debated topic.

illustrations have beguiled generation after generation of youngsters, but she was also a very keen naturalist with a very strong interest in mycology, the study of fungi. It is amazing to think that if it hadn't been for the inherent sexism of the times in which she lived, she might well have gone on to be remembered for her scientific studies as opposed to her creative works. In an oft-quoted letter, she wrote: 'You see, we do not believe in Schwendener's theory.'[10]

But regardless of whether or not Beatrix Potter believed it, Schwendener's theory was correct; lichens were indeed a combination of two very different things. However, the term 'dual hypothesis' that he coined to describe the relationship he had discovered didn't catch on, even when, in the following decade, more and more biologists gradually came around to his way of thinking. So it fell to another biologist to come up with the term that we use today. In 1877 the German scientist Albert Frank came up with the word 'symbiosis', and although he created it to describe the relationship between the algae and fungi forming lichen, it soon became the accepted term to describe a relationship between two different species.

Since then, the word has been hijacked somewhat, in that we humans tend to use it to describe positive interactions between ourselves as well, forgetting that we are actually the same species as each other. In this context we also use the word as a purely positive one, forgetting too that not all symbiotic relationships are positive for both participants, headlice and human beings providing a classic example of a symbiotic relationship that is far from being mutually beneficial.

Symbiotic relationships fall into three distinct main categories: mutualistic, parasitic or commensalistic. There are more categories, some of which are very technical, but here we shall stick with these three, because even they can get confusing.

We shall start by looking at parasitic relationships, as they are quite straightforward. A parasitic relationship is one in which one species exploits the other to the point that it gets benefit, whilst the other species suffers harm. The true definition of a parasitic relationship is where the species benefiting has actually adapted itself structurally to either live on or inside the species that is harmed. Tapeworms are an obvious, if unpleasant, example of a true parasitic relationship. Following that strict definition means that finding a true parasitic relationship between trees and birds is impossible.

A mutualistic relationship, as the name suggests, is one in which both participants mutually benefit from the interactions between them. In terms of trees and birds, an obvious example of this type of relationship is the one that exists between various species of hummingbird and various species of tropical tree. The small flying marvels that are hummingbirds feed on the tree's flowers, and in doing so they receive the nourishment they require to sustain themselves and their amazing flight capabilities. As they feed, the

---

10 The letter was to an amateur naturalist, Charles McIntosh. Beatrix Potter's mycological illustrations are exquisite and well worth seeking out.

Lichen on tree bark

flowers of the tree get pollinated, enabling the tree to set seed. Mutualistic relationships are generally pretty easy to recognise.

The third type of relationship is where it can start to all get a bit befuddling… A commensalistic relationship is one where one species gets a benefit whilst the other neither benefits from it or gets harmed by it. A bird nesting in the branches of a tree is an obvious example of a tree/bird relationship that can be labelled as commensalistic; the bird gets the benefit of a secure site to build its nest in, and the tree gets nothing. But what happens when the young in that nest are fed on insects, as they often are in small birds, and those insects are potentially harmful to the tree? This is where the areas start to become a bit grey. A good example of a small bird that nests within a tree and feeds its young on tree damaging insects is the great tit. When the young are being reared, a large proportion of what they are being fed are leaf-eating caterpillars. These larval insects can, in large numbers, defoliate trees, which obviously causes the tree a degree of harm, so perhaps the relationship in this case is more mutualistic. But the great tit nests in holes within the fabric of the tree, and they are quite good at chipping bits of wood off to enlarge either the entrance hole or the cavity within – something that could be argued as being harmful to the tree. But is it? And if it is, is it significant?

The problem with the classification of ecological relationships is that it is us humans that are producing these classifications. We love labels; we love putting things into an order of our own creation. We seem to have an overwhelming need to categorise everything in a way that we see as being best. We like neat and tidy. As lichens have already shown, nature doesn't necessarily fall in with our neat and orderly categorisations – but that of course doesn't stop us trying to shoehorn it in.

There is a form of commensalism that is used to describe hole-nesting birds: inquilinism. The word comes from the Latin for 'lodger' or 'tenant', so it describes a hole-nesting bird well – but inquilinism being a form of commensalism means that while the bird benefits from the relationship the tree has a neutral outcome from it. But then, what happens when that hole-nesting lodger is a woodpecker? Woodpeckers have a bill and a head structure that have evolved to do damage to wood, real damage to wood. Their young are also fed on insects, insects that can also cause real harm to trees, but for the woodpecker to get at those insects, it needs to quite literally hack parts of the tree apart to reach them. Parasitic relationships, as we have already seen, are when one species gets benefit whilst the other is harmed by the interaction. But to argue that the woodpecker's beak, stiff tail and toes (all of which are special adaptations for a life spent clinging to tree trunks) count as being structurally modified in the manner of a parasite is stretching the classification to incredulity. But then, how does the relationship between a woodpecker and a tree fit into our human-centric view of how these things are classified? Told you, the area's grey.

Personally, I am not sure that there is a fit for it, and it won't be the only relationship that doesn't fit into our own self-proclaimed order of life. Perhaps what we humans need to do is to accept that nature is nature and does what it does without any reference to how we think it should behave. But this doesn't mean it is any less interesting or fascinating– in fact, in my opinion it makes it all the better. We shall return to the subject of woodpeckers and trees. But for now, let's keep it simple.

Part Two
Commensalistic
happenings

Commensalistic happenings

A stairway to the heavens

Probably the most basic of relationships between the birds and the trees is the bird using the tree to get itself airborne. It is likely, as already mentioned previously, that this very basic interaction was perhaps the first between the trees and the creatures that would evolve into the birds we know today. This is a relationship that is most definitely commensalistic; the bird gets the benefit of a launch pad, and the tree is neither harmed nor benefited by it doing so.

For many birds, the act of getting into the air is difficult and energetically expensive, burning large amounts of valuable calories. If you have ever watched a mute swan taking off, you will know just how demanding taking to the air can be. These large white birds may be majestic as they glide gracefully through the water, but when trying to get airborne from it, they are a white blur of flapping wings and whirring legs, a moving mass of expending energy down a runway of water. There is nothing graceful about a swan taking to the air.

The launch-pad relationship between the trees and the birds is one that still occurs today, and although most flying birds have evolved the ability to get into the air unaided, some still need that helping hand, a step up if you like. The shearwaters are a group of magnificent birds, oceanic wanderers that are perfectly adapted to a life on the wing, flying vast distances across open seas, eschewing the land for a maritime existence. But like all birds, the necessities of breeding still tie them to that land that they would otherwise surely shirk. Shearwaters are a bit of a complicated group taxonomically, with several blurred lines when it comes to the birds being either subspecies or actual species – yet another example of how the natural world doesn't appear to easily fit into our neat and orderly way of seeing the world about us.

Whatever their taxonomic status, the shearwaters are generally long-winged birds, and in flight these wings have a distinctive stiff action to them. Their evocative group name comes from their manner of flying; the birds catch the updraft generated by waves and swells to minimise the physical effort they expend to stay airborne. They are the surfers of the air currents created by the waves. To fly like this, to catch the lift generated by the movement of the seas, they have to fly close to the water. To the human observers watching them from their ships many years ago, it appeared that the birds were so close to the seas that they were actually clipping, or shearing, the wave tops with their wings. They don't, of course, but the rather beautiful name of shearwater has stuck.

In light winds, when there is little movement in the seas below them, they are still able to fly close to the water's surface, employing a flapping and gliding flight technique that minimises effort. They are able to glide within a few centimetres of the surface, effectively floating on the air that is compressed between them and the water. It has been worked out that by flying in this manner, by using their bodies to compress the air beneath them on which they can then ride, they can save up to 80 per cent in energy expenditure compared to normal powered flight.[11]

One other characteristic feature of the shearwaters is that their legs are set far back on the body. They are used as a very effective underwater propulsion unit, pushing the bird like an outboard motor, the power generated enabling them to chase and catch their prey, sometimes to depths of over 50 metres. This positioning of the legs at the rear of the body is a feature shared by other unrelated birds that also pursue prey below the surface, birds like the divers, the grebes and the cormorants. But there is a trade-off. While rear-set legs may be useful for powering the bird through the water, they make the birds very ungainly on the land, giving them a tendency to shuffle along rather than actually walk. As a result, for many species of shearwater taking off from the ground is either very difficult or virtually impossible. This, of course, can lead them to being very vulnerable to predation by ground-dwelling mammalian predators, including ourselves.

Birds have evolved in all sorts of directions since that first interaction between them and the trees, but the one thing they all still have to do is lay their eggs, and as those eggs need incubation for the chicks to develop, that is something that cannot be done in water. When the divers and the grebes come to breed, they mitigate the risk of their vulnerability by constructing their nests in emergent vegetation in shallow water, keeping a watery margin between their nests and the land. The cormorants generally nest on inaccessible cliffs that are impossible for ground-dwelling mammals to access – but the shearwaters nest in burrows, and that means that they need to come onto land proper.

Shearwaters generally opt to nest on small offshore islands, establishing breeding colonies that they access at night to avoid the predatory interests of other birds like the gulls and the skuas. On the ground they are vulnerable, but these island sites are generally mammal-free (unless we in our wisdom have intervened), which means that they can stumble to and from their nest burrows without too much risk of being eaten. To return to their domain of the skies, many species of shearwaters launch themselves into the air by simply walking off the

---

11 Data adapted from *Weather and Bird Behaviour* by Norman Elkins, published by Poyser Books, 2004.

tops of the sheer cliffs on which their nest sites are located, opening their wings as they do so, capturing the lift and the currents of the air and sailing off through it. But one species still opts for the age-old method of using a tree to get airborne again, and that bird is the streaked shearwater.

Streaked shearwaters are birds of the wide open Pacific Ocean, roaming its vast waters and shearing the ocean's waves on their 1.2-metre wingspan, constantly on the lookout for the fish and squid on which they feed. They are relatively large members of the shearwater clan, with white underparts that contrast with grey-brown upper parts. The bird's principal breeding colonies are found on the many small offshore islands of Japan and the Korean peninsula, where it often breeds on forested slopes as opposed to bare clifftops. When these birds leave the confines of their nesting burrow, they don't head for the cliff edge to get back into the air; instead, they waddle and stumble their way along a network of well-worn pathways that lead to a particular tree. These are birds that need a tree to transform themselves from ungainly land stumbler to majestic aerial master.

Streaked shearwaters are not skilled tree climbers, but they are quite good tree clamberers, and the trees they select to use as their launch pads are carefully chosen to suit their arboreal skills. Invariably these trees are leaning specimens with angled trunks, enabling the birds to clamber up them without too much effort and struggle. But of course, trees leaning at just the right angle are at a premium, and once one is located it will be used by large numbers of the colony, year on year, generation after generation, each bird beating a path to it from its own nesting burrow, which can be many tens of metres away from the tree.

If you did not know about the streaked shearwater's lifestyle and you were to visit one of these breeding sites out of the bird's nesting season, you might find yourself somewhat perplexed by the labyrinth of well-worn pathways radiating from the base of a slightly leaning tree, a pattern of paths decorating the forest floor in all directions. But if you were to visit the tree at night during the breeding season, its importance to the birds would be all too obvious. The great David Attenborough, a man who very much played a part in getting me turned on to the wonders of wildlife through his brilliantly inspiring broadcasting career, visited such a site, and the footage recorded at the time shows the shearwaters waddling along the forest floor towards the tree before they then ascend it, one bird after another in an orderly procession, clambering upwards until they have reached sufficient height to step off the woody platform and open their proportionally very long wings. During the filming, one bird even stumbles as it clambers, slipping back down the trunk until it is stopped by Attenborough's arm; the bird, completely oblivious to the presence of the naturalist, uses the arm to push itself back up the tree trunk and continue its journey upwards.

The tree is evidently hugely important to the birds; if the tree was to topple it might even call into question the viability of that area of the nesting colony. Without a sufficiently suitable launching site the shearwaters would be forced to move location. This is an example of one of the most basic of tree/bird relationships, an interaction that must surely be a reflection of the first fledgling relationship that began millions and millions of years ago.

But just because the relationship between the shearwaters and the trees is a primeval one, it doesn't make it any less important – it's one that works, and one that has worked for millions of years. Those birds need those trees, and both the trees and the birds need us humans to understand that. Because without that understanding, a simple act on our part, the felling of just one tree, could jeopardise the future of the entire nesting colony.

An elevated position

While to begin with, all those millennia ago, trees may have been used by the birds as a gateway to the skies – an inclined runway that made take-off much easier – this would have also been opening up a whole world of other possibilities. One of the most obvious uses a tree brings, other than as a launch site, is that of elevation; a bird in a tree has a much better view of everything happening around it, the height providing the bird with increased opportunities for it to see both potential threats and, equally importantly, potential opportunities. Early birds would have readily exploited the advantage that a place in the tree's branches brought and, of course, their descendants still make use of elevated arboreal viewpoints today, using them to scour the ground below for prey, and to look out for possible predators, mates or territorial ingressors. Trees can be a place to advertise their presence from, or a place to seek refuge in.

If I think back to that bird I thought I saw all those years ago with my dad, I realise that I have developed a bit of an obsession for a group of birds that use trees in this way all the time. I might have been mistaken in my childhood enthusiasm to see a butcher bird that day, but since then I have seen lots and lots of shrikes. I never tire of watching them. Spending a lot of time in Extremadura in central Spain, I get to share a lot of my time with shrikes, in almost any habitat, be that on the edge of the village, or miles out into the countryside; there is usually one around somewhere.

Shrikes are a family of birds consisting of 34 species that are mainly found in Europe, Asia and Africa.[12] The shrikes are a group of birds that readily exploit trees as elevated perches to spot potential food from, and to keep an eye on what is happening in their environs. The two species found in the part of Extremadura where I dwell are the year-round resident Iberian grey shrike and the spring and summer-visiting woodchat shrike. Both use trees as perches, but they use them in subtly different ways.

The Iberian grey shrike is a beautiful bird, a blend of black, white and pinkish grey. An endemic of Iberia, it closely resembles the great grey shrike of northern Europe, but is darker and pinker, and has a lovely white line above its black eye mask that looks very much like an eyebrow, a feature that lends the bird bags of anthropomorphic character. It is the bigger of the two shrikes, and mainly feeds on large insects and small reptiles, both of which abound in Extremadura. It hunts by sitting exposed at the top of small trees, giving

12 There are two species that are found in North America, though: the loggerhead and the northern.

it a good vantage point from which to overlook a large area; it especially likes areas that are bare or short-turfed, scanning the terrain constantly for movement, and once prey is sighted, it will swoop quickly down to seize it.

Iberian grey shrike

The woodchat shrike is a stockier, shorter-tailed bird. There are no grey areas when it comes to the woodchat's plumage; it is a black-and-white kind of bird, albeit topped off with a lovely red crown and nape. A bit smaller than its relation, it mainly feeds on large insects and has a particular fondness for large dung beetles. It too uses trees as perches, but unlike its bigger cousin it tends to favour small dead branches at the bottom of the canopy. These perches, by the very nature of their location, are often in shade, and whilst that shade is probably welcomed by the bird in the fierce heat of an Extremaduran summer, it is also attractive to others.

Extremadura is known for its *dehesa*, a habitat that looks natural but is in fact a completely human-created agricultural system. Dehesa is wooded pasture, a combination of grassland and well-spaced woodland. The trees are mainly evergreen oaks, but cork oaks are also used where the conditions for this tree are more suitable. The trees are pruned every few years to retain tight, compact and low crowns which cast good amounts of shade onto the ground below; the system helps protect and retain the thin soils of the region, and it also provides much-needed shade for the livestock farmed within these vast acreages. Take a walk through an area of dehesa on a sunny summer's day and you will notice that all of the sheep will be congregated in groups within the cloak of shade afforded by the close canopies of the trees, seeking shelter from the relentless and unforgiving burning sun above.

Sheep produce copious amounts of dung, and when these ovine creatures concentrate in the shaded areas beneath the trees, the land they are on becomes ever more stercoraceous. So if you are a dung beetle this is the place to be, and if you eat dung beetles … The sheep produce dung and the dung beetles come to find it. The woodchat shrike, perched on its shady sub-canopy branch awaits them. There are many birds that use trees as hunting perches, of course – everything from raptors to flycatchers – but those two shrike species illustrate that even within the world of tree perches, there are different niches to be explored.

But the shrikes don't just use the trees as perches; they also use them as larders. As I have already mentioned, this group of birds are often colloquially known as butcher birds, a term that refers to their habit of impaling some prey items onto thorns as butchers hang meat. Nowadays, shrikes will readily use barbed wire fences to skewer their prey, but they didn't evolve this practice alongside the evolution of fences; they evolved it with spiny trees and shrubs. Many trees, higher than low-growing shrubs, offer the bird a secure storage spot away from inquisitive ground-dwelling mammals that will readily steal protein-packed food parcels.

There are many thoughts as to why shrikes impale some of their prey items; one commonly held thought is that the thorn or barb anchors the item, holding it still and allowing the bird to rip it apart with its bill. This certainly happens, but the birds are also quite capable of holding the item with their own feet whilst ripping it apart. A thorn or barb may assist in the process of dismemberment, but that doesn't appear to be the primary reason. The principal use of thorns to impale their prey items seems to be that of storage. These, then, are birds that are caching their food, stocking their larder if you like, perhaps taking advantage of a glut to see them through a lean period. But when it comes to explaining this behaviour there are more possibilities.

Many of the insect species caught by shrikes have evolved defences against being eaten that at best render them somewhat foul-tasting, or at worst leave them loaded with toxins. It has been suggested that hanging the dead corpse of the insect prey for a period before feeding on it gives sufficient time for those chemicals to break down and become less effective, and the prey more palatable.

Another possible reason is that the value of the food in terms of protein increases if the item is left to dry out in the fresh air. This is something that we humans have long understood; drying meat can allow it to improve nutritionally, the price of beef, for example, is much higher if it has been hung to dry for 28 days before being processed. (The dehesas of Extremadura are also used to rear pigs to produce the famous hams of the region; these hams are cured uncooked meat, left to hang for several months and even years, the ones that have hung the longest deemed the most flavoursome and therefore the most valuable.) Recent studies have shown that perhaps shrikes too understand the value of hung food. Male shrikes, when trying to solicit a mating with a female, will routinely present her with a meal. But the studies indicate that they present her with food that they have already impaled, rather than a freshly caught item – and furthermore, it would seem as if they deliberately select items that have been impaled for the optimum amount of time, as opposed to one impaled only a few hours earlier. This implies that the shrikes know the value of the hung meat, the male using it to try and impress the female, and the female assessing the male on the quality of the food he offers.

Birds using trees as hunting perches is a simple enough interaction between the two. Even birds storing food on the spines of trees is an interaction that is pretty basic at face value, but, like many things, when you look closer at the reasons for something happening, the more you ask 'Why?' the more intrigue you discover. The relationship between shrikes and trees is a commensalistic one – it is the bird that is getting all the benefit – but even so, by looking closer, we are still able to discover some amazing things.

Shrikes may perch in trees and subsequently use them to store food that they have spotted from the branches, but there is another bird that uses its arboreal viewing point not to store food, but to subdue it. The common kingfisher is a real birding gem. It may be small,[13] but it is surely one of the most colourful birds of the British Isles, a mixture of orangey-red, greenish-blue and a stunning electric blue back best seen when the bird's zipping low over a river, a bright tracer bullet amidst a blur of fast-action wings.

Kingfishers are capable of hovering over water when looking for food, but by far the most popular way for them to spot their prey is to sit motionless on a perch over the water.

---

13 I often find that non-birders are surprised at how small these avian delights are when they actually see them, I think it's because any picture of a kingfisher in a book or a magazine invariably fills the page, maximising the bird's beauty. So these pictures tend to be considerably bigger than the bird itself.

I have a spot that I go to regularly that is almost guaranteed to yield me one of these birds; a slow-flowing stretch of river with a number of riverside trees, most of which have low thin branches that hang out over the water. One tree in particular, a rather haggard goat willow, has a long thin branch that seems especially favoured by these kings of fishers.

I have often watched a kingfisher perched on this branch, its bill pointing downwards as the bird sits still, intently observing the shallow waters below. The shade of the tree obscures the bird's colouration, until it suddenly drops off the perch and that brilliant blue flashes in the sunlight before becoming lost amongst the explosion of diamond-like water droplets as the bird follows its dagger of a beak through the surface. The act of catching the fish is all a bit too fast for us to follow; before you know it the bird is back up on the branch holding its catch tightly in its bill. The catcher doesn't immediately eat the caught, though; before consuming the still-living fish, the bird manoeuvres the unfortunate minnow[14] to hold it near the tail, then swings its own head violently to smack the head of the fish hard against the branch several times to kill it or at the very least stun it. The kingfisher, then, is a bird that doesn't just use a tree as a perch from which to spot its prey, it also uses the tree as a weapon.

Other species of bird use tree branches to prepare their prey in a slightly different way to the kingfisher. The European bee-eater is another colourful birding beauty. Sadly it is not a British breeder,[15] but if you have been to southern Europe in the summertime you are very likely to have seen these flying rainbows. The bird's name tells you pretty much everything you need to know about its feeding habits; it eats a variety of flying insects, but it particularly likes bees, wasps and hornets. Its food comes with a literal sting in the tail.

Bee-eaters pluck the insects out of the air using their tweezer-like bills – bills that are long enough to hold the snatched insect away from the face, avoiding the risk of being stung. But swallowing an insect with a sting is a sure way of getting stung. Bee-eaters like perching on dead branches that offer them a vantage point that they can use to spot their prey, but they use these branches to process the prey as well. The bird holds the insect by the head or thorax, then smears the end of the abdomen, where the sting is housed, along the bare branch of the tree repeatedly, until the sting is dislodged and the meal rendered safe. The bird is deliberately using the tree to process its food. Bee-eaters don't just eat stinging insects; they also eat others such as butterflies. But the birds don't process these species, as they recognise that they don't have any hazards that need to be dislodged. The birds use the trees for a specific purpose when dealing with a specific species.

Like the shrike using fences to store the food it catches, the bee-eater will also use fence posts and walls to remove the stings of its prey, but as with the aforementioned butcher birds, this is behaviour that evolved long before we built these structures; indeed, this has

---

14 I use the word 'minnow' here in its generalised meaning; kingfishers will catch a wide range of small fish species.

15 Occasional pairs do try, though, and it is possible that this is a bird that might slowly colonise Britain in years to come.

been happening most probably long before we even existed. The bee-eater will have evolved its food-processing behaviour with the trees that act as perches for it.

Birds perched in trees may be doing so to look for food; they may be doing so to rest without fear of predation from land-based mammals; they may also be using the elevation of the tree to broadcast their song far and wide, exploiting the procerity of the tree to allow their communicative music to be heard over relatively large distances, unhindered by the muffling effects of ground-based objects. There are a plethora of reasons why birds perch in trees, and the act of doing so was a natural progression in the developing relationship between birds and trees that started all those millions of years ago.

From using trees to get airborne through to using them to perch in or even to kill or process their prey, the next step in the ever-developing relationship between the birds and the trees was probably the use of the trees by birds as secure sites in which they could breed.

Nests

If we go back to that classic child's drawing of a lollipop tree, we may find that the child added, with undoubted artistic flourish, a bird's nest tucked into the rounded ball of the tree's canopy. As we all know, birds make their nests in all sorts of places, be that in grasses, on bare ground, on floating platforms on water, on cliff ledges, even underground – but it is in trees that we tend to place the typical image of a bird nesting.

Nesting in a tree is a logical thing to do if you are a bird in a land inhabited by ground-dwelling mammals, and whilst many predatory mammals can climb trees, they are limited by weight and agility when it comes to reaching the outer, thinner branches in which some nests are built. Bigger birds tend to nest in bigger branches, often close to the tree's trunk; this might make them more vulnerable, but these bigger birds have the defence of attack. A mammal climbing a vertical trunk doesn't have a lot of scope to defend itself if an angry dive-bombing bird like a crow is launching an attack at it. Loosening its grip to fend off the bird, or even attack it, is likely to lead to the would-be nest robber going down in the world. Rapidly and painfully.

Many, many species of birds use trees in which to build their nest structures, from the very small to the gargantuan. The world's smallest bird, the stunningly beautiful bee hummingbird, a refractive mix of iridescence, builds its tiny nest in the branches of trees in its native land of the island of Cuba, somehow weaving together spider webs, fragments of bark and pieces of lichen to make a delicate cup-shaped structure that measures just 2.5 cm across. At the opposite end of the spectrum, one of world's biggest flying birds, the old world black vulture,[16] also constructs its nest in trees, but there is nothing delicate about this construction; it gathers up a plethora of large sticks to build a platform around 2 metres in diameter. This nest gets used year after year by these long-lived birds, and each

---

16 With a wingspan of just under 3 metres, these are huge birds.

year they refurbish it, adding yet more material to the already bulky mass, so after a while not only does the nest grow in expanse but it also takes on great depth, sometimes up to as much as 3 metres. Like the nest of the bee hummingbird, the nest of the black vulture also contains spider webs, but the difference is that they haven't been used by the vulture to bind the nest together, in fact the vulture has had nothing to do with their presence other than through creating a structure that is so large it has become a mini-habitat in its own right. All sorts of things live within a black vulture nest, the spiders making their webs in them to catch the myriad insects that are also using them. Black vulture nests are an ecosystem all by themselves. I have never seen a bee hummingbird's nest, although it is a bird I really want to see, so maybe one day I will, but I have seen plenty of black vulture nests, and they really are colossal structures.

But they aren't the biggest tree nests; the largest tree-built bird nest recorded to date belonged to a pair of bald eagles in the state of Florida in America. Like the black vultures of Europe, these birds are long-lived and will reuse their nest year after year, adding to its bulk each time. In 1963 the Florida nest was measured by biologists, and the dimensions recorded were remarkable; this giant of a nest came in at just under 3 metres across and just over 6 metres deep, and it weighed in at an estimated 2.7 tonnes – that's heavier than a Land Rover Discovery.

This amazing size record is one that has some stiff competition, but not from a similar-sized bird; the competition comes from a much, much smaller bird, the sociable weaver. This African bird is the same size as the more familiar house sparrow– it even looks a bit like one – it's tiny in comparison to the iconic bald eagle, but just because it's small doesn't mean that it doesn't have grand designs when it comes to nest building. This small bird, just a few centimetres long and a few grams in weight, builds one of the largest and most spectacular nest structures of any bird anywhere in the world, although it doesn't do so on its own. As the name suggests, sociable weavers are not lone workers; they are cooperative builders that undertake community housing projects.

Whilst the bald eagles build their nests together as a pair, the sociable weavers build theirs as a large group, creating a wonderful-looking structure that can house well over 100 pairs of these small birds. Some birds build nests; sociable weavers build villages.

Most nests built in trees have no impact on the tree itself; this is perhaps the classic example of a commensalistic relationship, the bird benefiting from the structural support of the tree's form to help it construct its nest, whilst the tree itself gains no benefit nor does it suffer any disadvantage from the presence of the nest.

But the presence of a nest or nests in a tree isn't always benign for the tree. When the nests are as large as the ones mentioned above, they can and do have serious implications for the tree they are built in. Large nests can create an increase in what arborists term 'wind sail'; the amount of surface area of, and within, a tree that catches the wind, just as a sail does on a boat. The greater this wind sail area, the greater the chance of the wind catching it in such a way as to damage the tree or even, in the worst of cases, to blow the whole tree over. There is also the weight factor to consider; a nest that weighs in at just under 3 tonnes is a nest that is going to be putting incredible strain on the branches it is built upon – and this strain can, and often does, lead to breakages within the ramified structure of the tree.

White stork nest

But even if an individual nest is of a size which doesn't dangerously increase the wind sail factor, or put excessive strain on the branches it is built upon, if these individual nests form a colony within a single tree there can be other serious implications for that tree. Birds such as cattle egrets, white storks and some species of heron build their scruffy stick nests in trees, often in loose colonies; sometimes it appears to us as if one tree among many is the one chosen by the birds to build their nests in, all the other trees around seemingly shirked as the birds concentrate their nest building in just this single specimen. It isn't this concentration of nests that is necessarily problematic for the tree, but the concentration of other things.

If you have ever visited an active heronry or an active rookery[17] of egrets or even a breeding colony of storks, one of the first things you'll notice is the smell. All of these birds produce copious amounts of droppings, and at nesting time these droppings are concentrated in the immediate area. If there are a dozen nests in a tree, then there is going to be a lot of bird poo concentrated in and around that tree. Bird poo of these species (and others[18]) is a concentrated mix of various salts and ammonia, none of which are very good for the tree. Concentrated ammonia can kill trees outright, but even in lesser amounts it will scorch leaves and lead to defoliation in the part of the tree around the nest. The continuous accumulation of droppings on the ground below the tree can also lead to high levels of ammonia and salts leaching into the soil, where they are ultimately taken up by the tree's roots, poisoning the tree over time.

Even without all the chemicals in it, the thick white droppings cause problems for the tree by coating the leaves, in effect painting them with poo. This shuts out the sunlight from the surface of the leaf, therefore shutting down the photosynthesising factory that a leaf is. If this happens to a large number of leaves, then it too can adversely affect the health of the tree, sometimes leading to an entire branch dying off because its leaves have been covered. But even if the coverage isn't total, the reduction in photosynthesising may lead to the tree becoming less able to defend itself against pathogens, rendering it more vulnerable to disease. Tree-nesting birds can be more than innocuous lodgers.

But most nests built by birds in trees, especially in Britain, are of a size and a number that don't threaten the tree in any way.[19] Nests at their most basic are platforms exploiting the layout of the tree's branches that offer these structures the support they require. At other times, though, the nests can be woven into the small branches themselves, suspended in the trees rather than sitting on them, improbably held fast by the bird's ingenious dexterity. Other nests can be tucked under damaged areas of bark, wedged into crevices; they can even be located down amongst the roots. The trees offer a wide range of opportunities for birds to build a wide range of nests, but perhaps the most interesting example of an arboreal nesting opportunity is the hole.

---

17 The somewhat confusing name for an egret nesting colony.

18 The cormorant is another species that when nesting in trees can cause problems with its droppings.

19 There are exceptions, though; with the increasing numbers of egrets breeding in Britain and the potential gradual colonisation by white storks, it is likely that there will be more examples of the poo effect on trees.

Wholly natural

The natural formation of holes in trees is something that happens all the time. The hole's creation can be a part of the tree's growing process, a way of recycling and remodelling itself throughout its life. Sometimes, though, the formation of holes can be the result of a wound; strong winds and bad weather can literally rip holes in a tree's superstructure, creating a plethora of opportunities for nesting birds. Whether holes are created by the tree itself or caused by external sources like the weather, holey trees are a natural part of healthy woodland.

If you take a cross-section of a tree trunk, it is only the very outer edge that is actually living tissue. The centre of the tree, the timber we often so highly value, is quite literally dead wood. And just as a business trying to economise will look to get rid of any metaphorical dead wood it is carrying, a tree will sometimes look to get rid of the literal dead wood it is carrying.

As a young tree is growing, the timber heartwood of the trunk provides it with a solid core, a rigid central column that supports the tree in its growth, helping it to withstand outside forces such as wind. But as the tree gets older and reaches maturity, that solid core will have become a bit superfluous. The tree's root system will by now have securely anchored it into the ground, greatly reducing any risk of the tree toppling over. The now substantial bulk of the central core will no longer be as important to the tree as it once was, and the need to retain the core in its entirety will have diminished. The tree's trunk still needs to be rigid, strong enough to stop any buckling or collapse, but it doesn't need to be solid.

It's not just birds that trees form relationships with; they form relationships with a whole host of life forms, and arguably the most important of these relationships are the ones that they form with fungi. We have only recently started to appreciate the importance and significance of these highly complicated and involved interactions. A tree growing in a wood isn't a lone entity – it's a fully plugged-in member of the woodwide web of life, and it's the fungi that provide the necessary wiring.

This isn't the book to explore the vital importance of these vital tree–fungus relationships, but suffice to say a woodland can only function truly and healthily with these relationships in place. One of the many interactions between the two involves the transfer and supply of nutrients, food. As the trees mature so the fungi start to break down the old heartwood within them, consuming the lignin and other materials within the wood that are otherwise difficult to break down. This process releases long-tied-up nutrients, either into the soil or directly passed back to the tree via the fungal hyphae network which connects into the tree's root system. The dead wood is being recycled. We used to look at fungi in woodlands as being a potential threat to the trees – and to be fair there are a few that are a threat, including the infamous honey fungus[20] – but the vast majority of fungus species present in a woodland form symbiotic relationships with the trees, relationships that the trees need.

The result of this recycling is that trees as they mature start to hollow out, which is why it can be incredibly difficult to accurately age truly old trees in most parts of the world.[21] The process of a tree developing a hollow centre as it ages is a perfectly natural phenomenon. It doesn't mean the tree is dying – indeed, the vast majority of our largest and oldest trees in Britain have had hollow centres for hundreds of years. It has even been suggested that this hollowing out could actually help old trees survive significant weather events such as severe winds, with the hollow nature of the main stem allowing the tree to flex in the sudden gusts where a completely rigid stem would be more likely to fail by snapping. Mature trees are not necessarily solid trees.

These hollow stems can and do provide nest sites for bird species, but it is usually holes on a smaller scale that we think of when we think of birds nesting within a tree as opposed to on it. Many of us have bird boxes in our gardens; these boxes are in effect fake tree holes, mimics of the nesting habitat that is naturally created as trees grow. In many situations the lack of naturally occurring tree holes reduces the ability of birds to nest in an area, potentially limiting their range and distribution as a result. Modern forestry is a classic example; the trees are harvested when they reach economic maturity as opposed to actual maturity,[22] so in commercial timber plantations the trees don't have the time to develop holes, and as a result, most commercial forestry plantations hold far fewer numbers of breeding birds than the equivalent area of non-commercial woodland, even where the tree species is the same in both. The provision of bird boxes in plantations can go a long way to helping the bird (and bat) populations in these plantations, and their use in such situations should be greatly expanded.

---

20 The honey fungus species, and there are at least ten, are some of the biggest living organisms on the planet, with one in the USA recorded as being 3.4 square miles in extent.

21 The famously old bristlecone pines in the Rockies grow in such a harsh, arid and cold environment that the natural processes of the trees are slowed right down, and the trees haven't hollowed, allowing them to be accurately aged by ring-counting techniques. But these are the exception.

22 When foresters talk about tree maturity, they are often doing so from a timber-growing perspective. This is very different from actual age maturity. A tree reaching timber or economic maturity is usually quite young. A Sitka spruce grown in Britain can reach timber or economic maturity in 50 years, but these trees can live for many centuries, with some even believed to be 1,000 years old. *That* is mature.

Another artificial habitat where nest boxes can provide an important nesting resource is in gardens and urban areas. Most gardens are lacking in large mature trees in which holes have naturally developed, yet many of us revel in the joy birds bring us when they visit them. Putting up a bird box, or better still, a number of bird boxes, in a garden is not only a great thing to do for the birds that visit your garden – it's also a great thing to do for yourself. The joy of watching birds rear a brood in a box in your garden is one of the best feel-good medications there is.[23]

The typical bird box that we all recognise is the small hole-fronted box. The vast majority of nest boxes that are commercially available are of this type, and they provide a home for a variety of bird species that regularly use our gardens and their feeders. In my own garden I have had blue tit, great tit, house sparrow and nuthatch use this type of box; the sparrows are opportunists and will seemingly nest anywhere (including in our thatched roof), but the tits and the nuthatch are primarily woodland birds, and these boxes mimic the typical tree hole found in woodland.

Nuthatch and bird box

---

23 See Appendix 2 for a design template for a basic hole-nesting box that mimics a natural tree hole site. Every garden needs a bird box!

As trees grow they produce branches, but as the tree develops and gets bigger, as it interacts with neighbouring trees around it, some of these branches lose their purpose and become redundant. This often happens when the branches have been shaded out by either the tree's own branches above or by the branches of other, nearby trees. Once these branches become redundant, the tree will typically start to begin a process to shed them.

If the branches are small, generally no more than a couple of centimetres in diameter, the tree will carry out a process that we call cladoptosis. This process is pretty much identical to that of abscission, the method used by a deciduous tree to shed its leaves in the autumn. Trees are very thrifty – they never waste resources – so the first thing that happens is something called resorption; this is where the tree breaks down any available nutrients within the branch that it can then reabsorb into the tissues of the main stem. Once this has been completed, once the branch has been drained of anything salvageable, the tree acts to completely seal it off by laying down a layer of cork cells. These are then strengthened by the addition of lignin to form a waterproof boundary, effectively cutting the branch off.

The small branch is now nothing more than a dead branch hanging, waiting for either the weather, an animal or general decomposition to cause it to drop. If you walk through a young commercial conifer plantation once the trees have closed the canopy, you will see examples of cladoptosis all around you. The small, brittle sticks arranged in whorls around the lower trunks are the result of this process; former branches with photosynthesising needles on, they have been starved of light by the tree's growth, lost their purpose and become nothing more than a burden, and as a result the tree has initiated the process to discard them. As the conifers mature, their stems become 'clean' (a forestry term that means they are free of branches), but the shadows of these small branches can still be found in the timber within the trunks, in the form of knots.

Because the branches involved in cladoptosis are small, their loss doesn't lead to holes forming; the trunk of the tree is sealed off and the branch falls within a few months. For a tree and its timescales, this is a relatively quick process. But for a hole to form, the branch needs to be bigger and the process needs to take longer. When a branch is big, the process of cladoptosis doesn't work; for a tree to shed one of these branches it needs to undertake something that arborists call natural pruning.

When we decide to prune a tree it is a quick process; a few snips here and a few snips there, and the job is generally done. But trees operate at a different rate to us humans. They live their long lives at a slower pace than we do, so when trees prune themselves it can be a process that takes several years, even decades, to complete. One of the trees that regularly prunes itself as it grows is the pedunculate oak, the so-called English oak, a tree familiar to us all. It is one that we can easily find growing around us in both rural and urban settings, and if you find a medium to large one you should be able to spot various stages of natural pruning happening within its canopy just by looking up.

The photo below shows a typical example of a pedunculate oak growing alongside a lane in mid-Devon; although it is near woodland, it is an example that has always grown alone, its low, large spreading limbs testament to this. As this tree has grown it has produced many branches that have become superfluous to it as other branches developed above and around them, so to save energy and redistribute important resources, the tree has pruned itself on several occasions.

Open-grown oak

When the branch to be discarded is larger than a couple of centimetres in diameter, the process to remove it takes time, and several years will pass before the branch is completely lost. As in cladoptosis the tree will seal the original trunk/branch junction with the cork cells reinforced with lignin, severing the flow of sap to the branch, and this rapidly (in tree terms!) kills the branch. But because the branch is large it takes a long time for it to degrade and rot or become brittle enough to be knocked off. During this time the tree is not dormant, nor is it awaiting the demise of the branch before it carries on; the tree is continuing to grow.

As we all know, trees, in the temperate zones at least, lay down annual rings as part of their growth, expanding in girth and volume each annual cycle. Because the removal of a branch can take years to complete, the tree will have grown out around the now-dead branch with several years of new growth. This effectively swallows up the first part of the branch, subsumed by the increasing girth of the trunk or large branch it was originally growing from. But because the remnant branch is still there, the new growth has to grow around what is now in effect a foreign body. This causes callusing, a swelling of new tissue around the wound of dead wood. This can be seen in the photo opposite that shows the same tree as before. The wood of the old branch has started to degrade and has slowly diminished in size; it is now nothing more than a piece of dead wood sticking out of the tree's trunk. If you look at the point where the dead branch meets the trunk you will clearly see the swelling surrounding it.

As the dead branch slowly degrades, each year that goes by leads to another layer of new wood being laid down around it; this new wood forms what is known as a trunk collar around the old branch, a ring of growth that completely encircles it. The illustration opposite shows how this process occurs. When the dead wood of the old branch finally rots away or falls off, it leaves a socket of callused growth around where it once grew: a hole. The tree will attempt to seal this hole by laying down new growth where the branch bark ridge is, gradually reducing the diameter of the hole as its rim thickens; the tree doesn't want the hole to be there, it wants to seal it to help protect the integrity of its stem. But, again, it is not a quick process; it can take decades, and because it takes so long and because the tree will be naturally pruning itself of other branches during this time there will be other holes being formed as the first one closes.

There is a constant succession of holes being formed and closed on mature trees, but it is something that happens incredibly slowly from our point of view, which is why we don't often appreciate that it is continually happening – but happen it does. The photos on page 54 show the same tree as before; the first shows a typical tree hole that has developed as a result of the oak naturally pruning itself. You can clearly see that the swelling around the hole is the same as the swelling around the base of the dead branch in the previous picture, the only difference being that this branch has now gone, leaving behind the socket it once sat within. The second photo shows the dead branch a metre or so away from the hole; most mature oaks will have these features on them. This particular tree had several examples of the self-pruning process, from dying branch through to a nest-perfect hole.

The larger the hole's diameter when the old branch finally goes, the deeper the socket will be in the tree's trunk or large branch. This variety of hole and socket sizes in turn has led to a variety of different birds that will use them to nest in, from the typical woodland tits through to jackdaws and owls. The holes make great nest sites for birds, as they are secure places in which to rear a brood, protected by hard callused walls of wood. The only weak point is the entrance itself, but the bird will mitigate this risk by selecting a hole that is only just big enough for itself. A blue tit won't select a large nest hole to breed in, because if it did, larger birds could enter and predate the eggs or the young; instead it will select a hole that it can just fit through. This also excludes competition from bigger relatives like the great tit, which might evict the smaller bird from a hole that it could use. Species fill niches in ecosystems, and one of the key niches for birds is the availability of suitable nest sites. The variety of bird species that use holes in which to breed indicates just how normal and common it is for trees to develop holes as part of their natural growing patterns. There is nothing unnatural about holey trees.

Old dead branch on oak, showing collar

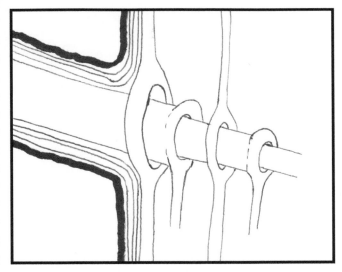

Illustration showing the formation of trunk collars around the branch as annual growth rings are laid down. It is this formation of trunk collars that forms the branch socket which has the potential to become a natural tree hole for birds to exploit as a nest resource.

But the hole is not a static, fixed object; the tree is trying to close it, to seal it and protect itself, finishing off the act of natural pruning that it had started, sometimes many years before. But there are other processes at play as well, processes that will slow, or even prevent, the closure of the hole. The inside of the hole is at risk of rotting; this can be exacerbated by a location on the tree that may expose it directly to rain or to water run-off flowing down the trunk. This can lead to the hole, and the cavity within, becoming bigger, potentially to the advantage of bigger birds. The nesting birds play a part too, I have often watched blue and great tits peck away at the entrance hole to nest boxes and have also seen plenty of evidence of them enlarging the cavity within by using their bills to excavate the sides. Nuthatches, too, are very adept at enlarging holes; their dagger of a beak is a formidable chisel and they will enlarge a smaller hole rapidly so that they can easily fit into it.[24] As the tree tries to close the hole, the birds of various species can often be found trying to maintain it as an opening.

Naturally occurring tree hole with swelling.

The tree hole on the right and the dead branch undergoing self-pruning on the left.

Birds like the blue tit are a great species of bird for the oak to have nearby because every spring the leaves of the oak are assailed and assaulted by hordes of defoliating caterpillars – caterpillars which are a key food of blue tits when they are rearing their young. Because of this, it has been inferred in the past that the holes in trees have been 'provided' for the tits to nest in so that they are then on hand to deal with the caterpillars – that in other words a bird such as a blue tit nesting in a hole in an oak tree is an example of a mutualistic relationship, the bird benefiting from the safe nesting space, and the tree benefiting from its tenant, the bird, feeding on defoliating insects.

24 Conversely, nuthatches will also use their beaks to make holes smaller if they judge them too large; this time, though, the beak is not used as a chisel, but as a plasterer's trowel. The bird collects wet mud and uses it to plaster up the hole to reduce its diameter. If they are using a nest box they will sometimes even plaster any gaps around the edge of the lid as well.

But the holes aren't provided for the birds; they are a result of the natural growth patterns of the tree; growth rings are laid down that increase the girth and volume of the tree, even around dead and decaying branches, and it is this that forms the holes. Trees were already growing in this way for millions of years before modern birds evolved, and the birds have taken advantage of the trees' natural growth patterns. The birds have evolved to exploit the plethora of nesting opportunities that have arisen from trees growing, but the two did not evolve together.

Our problem is we tend to look at something in much the same way as we look at a photo; it's a moment in time that we are looking at, and we don't necessarily see the bigger picture – what's happening before and after the photo was taken. As we look at it in the moment, we may indeed be able to see a blue tit taking a beakful of oak-defoliating caterpillars into the hole to feed its brood of hungry young, and in this moment it does make sense to us that a tree might provide a nest hole for this insectivorous bird. But what we are *not* seeing is the fact that the tree, slowly but surely, is working to seal that hole up, to remove it – and the nesting opportunity it brings – completely. The photo below shows exactly what the tree is trying to achieve.

Sealed tree hole

Birds nesting in tree holes are not an example of a mutualistic relationship. No matter how tempting it is to think that it is, it is in fact a commensalistic one, and as we have already seen, it is one with its own name, inquilinism; the birds are lodgers as opposed to partners. There are examples of mutualistic relationships between the trees and the birds, and we will get to them later on, but before we do there are a couple of other topics in the birds-nesting-in-trees area that we shall look at.

First up, it is back to that grey area of tree-hole-nesting birds, the fabulous woodpeckers.

Woodpeckers

For 20 years of my working life I was a forest ranger; this inevitably meant that I spent a lot of my time immersed in various forests, and in those forests, in amongst the millions of trees, I frequently encountered a group of birds that must surely do nothing but damage trees. The woodpeckers are a group of birds that are well known to pretty much everybody; even if someone has never seen an actual living woodpecker, they are sure to know that these carpenters of the woods use their chisel-like bills to make holes in the wooden stems of trees.

As we shall see later, some birds do indeed form mutually beneficial relationships with trees – but surely the woodpeckers are nothing more than arboreal vandals, causing damage as opposed to benefit.

But are they? Are we misjudging the woodpecker when we think of them and their relationships with the trees? Just because many species of woodpecker are black and white, it doesn't mean that the same goes for their relationship with trees. Surprisingly, for a group of birds so well known generally, there is still much that we don't know about them specifically. We are not even sure exactly how many species there actually are, and for a couple of the largest species, we aren't even sure if they still exist or not.[25] In his book *Woodpecker*, the renowned expert on these birds, Gerard Gorman, states that the number of extant species within this family of birds lies between 225 and 250. The reason for the uncertainty regarding the actual species numbers is that taxonomically there is still much to be resolved.

Woodpeckers are found throughout the world, absent only from the continents of Antarctica, where there are no trees, and Oceania (Australia, New Zealand, Papua New Guinea and the islands of the Pacific). They are also absent from some of the more remote islands in the world, such as Madagascar. In Europe we have nine resident species and one migratory species, the not very woodpeckerlike wryneck. Of the nine residents, three species are present in Britain, the beautiful green, the familiar great spotted and the – sadly increasingly rare – lesser spotted. The atypical wryneck used to breed in Britain, but despite it being recorded as being numerous in the early 19th century, this beautifully and cryptically plumaged bird declined rapidly as we drastically altered the structure of the countryside and how we managed it, this small woodpecker ceasing to be a regular breeder here by the 1970s.

---

25 The ivory-billed woodpecker and the closely related imperial woodpecker hopefully are, but more probably were, the largest of the woodpecker species. Sadly, both are now believed to be extinct.

When I first started working in forestry, an older colleague described our commonest species, the great spotted woodpecker, as a tree destroyer, firmly believing that their activities killed healthy (and therefore potentially profitable) trees. I can remember clearly the first time he used that phrase to refer to one of these black-and-white avian delights; it was not what I'd expected to hear as we stood in the forest watching the bird scramble around the trunk of a tree to hide from us. The fact that my colleague had spent several decades working in forests, knew the forest and its inhabitants intimately, yet had still got the ecology of one of our commonest woodland birds completely wrong was a bit of a shock for me – an avian case of not seeing the wood for the trees, perhaps?

The truth is that although great spotted woodpeckers, like most (see below) other woodpeckers, don't kill trees at all, there is a common and widespread perception that they do, even amongst people who should know better. Great spotted woodpeckers are hole-nesters, but unlike the majority of other species that nest in holes they have the capability to actually excavate their nest chamber themselves, using their chisel-like bill and specially evolved shock-absorbing head and neck structure to do so. But they generally choose dead wood in which to carry out their carpentry excavations, rather than healthy – and much more solid – wood.

If you walk through a 30-year-old (or older) forestry plantation in Britain you are very likely to come across a dead tree that has one or more woodpecker nest holes chiselled into it. These trees are often no more than 'snags', snapped-off tree trunks shorn of their upper half and canopy. They are mere remnants of trees, but despite their decay and broken appearance they still stand in their place within the serried ranks of the planted plantation. These dead trees, though, weren't killed by woodpeckers excavating their nests within their trunks; instead it's because the trees were already dead that the woodpeckers will have chosen them in the first place to excavate their nests in. The birds have simply taken advantage of the softer wood present in these dead stems.

Unfortunately there are people – and my old colleague was surprisingly one of them – that fall into the trap of seeing a dead tree complete with woodpecker holes, and jumping to the wrong conclusion when it comes to cause and effect. But, if you look closely at what you are seeing, the evidence showing this not to be the case is all too evident. In a stand of 30-year-old Scots pine, the uniformity of the trees is immediately obvious; they are a crop and have therefore been grown to a rigid format to ensure that they produce viable timber that we, the consumer, will buy and use. After all, when we go to the shop to buy timber for a DIY project, we want straight, non-knotty wood, and it is the forestry plantation system that produces this timber. Often, the only non-conformity within this crop of trees is a solitary dead snag, gradually falling to pieces, recycling itself back into the soil. It will be this epitaph of a tree that has the hallmarks of woodpecker-nesting activity carved into it. None of the other, living, trees will.

Great Spotted Woodpecker,
photo used with kind permission of Stuart Gillies.

These snags can have several woodpecker holes in them, the number depending on the length of time that they have been dead. Great spotted woodpeckers are territorial birds – not birds that nest colonially – and they won't tolerate another pair trying to nest near them. So each hole you see in a snag signifies one breeding year for one pair of birds. They may re-use an old hole and chamber the following year, but the conifer species that make up our plantations break down relatively quickly once dead, so the birds often have to make a new hole and chamber each year. As the standing dead wood degrades further, the security it offers for nesting within it also degrades, but in a conifer plantation this may be the only site available for the birds to breed in. If the great spotted woodpecker was indeed a tree destroyer, as my old colleague thought, it wouldn't carry on trying to nest in a crumbling dead stem, but would simply excavate another one in a living tree. The solitary snags are heavily drilled because there is an unnatural lack of snags and dead wood in commercial forestry plantations, and this lack of dead wood limits the birds. If they were able to, they would no doubt create more nest sites in much more secure timber – but they can't and they don't. These birds aren't tree destroyers, nor are they arboreal vandals; they are filling their ecological niche, and they do so by nesting in standing dead wood.

But what about when it comes to the bird's feeding habits? The European woodpeckers are primarily invertebrate feeders. Within the group of European species, the green woodpecker, the closely related grey-headed woodpecker of central and Eastern Europe, and the unusual wryneck favour ants for their food – but the other species feed on a variety of insects that generally spend their larval stages in wood. These young insects spend their time boring their way through the tree's tissues, effectively eating the tree from the inside out, before pupating and then emerging as adults to mate and start the process again. To access this nutritious grub grub, the woodpecker needs to be able to get at them – and it has, of course, the perfect tool with which to do so. Woodpeckers will peck away at the living tissue of trees to get at the insects within, and this causes what we could easily refer to as damage – but as Gerard Gorman pointed out to me, it is best to avoid using the word 'damage' because of the connotations that we associate with it. In Gerard's own words, *'woodpeckers don't kill trees, fungi and insects do. When woodpeckers start to peck into trees they are already ill or dead'*.

That said, there is a branch of the woodpecker family in the Americas that can and does kill trees in its quest for the food source that has given the four species in the *Sphyrapicus* genus their common name, sapsucker. Instead of using their bills to find insects chewing away inside the tree, they use them to chisel holes in the bark to access the tree's sap. But they don't just make one hole to do so – they make lots and lots; sometimes a tree can be peppered with hundreds of small holes, and if these holes form a ring around the tree's circumference it will girdle the tree and kill it.[26] Clearly this group of woodpeckers and their preference

---

26 Girdling is also known as ring barking. If a ring of bark is removed down to the wood around the entire circumference of the trunk, everything above this wound will die as the vessels supplying the leaves with water are severed. Some tree species are able to send up new growth from below this wound, but others, particularly conifers, are unable to do so, and die.

for a sugary sweet liquid diet can be injurious to trees. However, the European species of woodpecker much prefer to feed on insects that are themselves harmful to the trees.

Not every culture portrays how woodpeckers feed as being damaging to the trees they are feeding on; in eastern Europe many children grow up learning that woodpeckers are the doctors of the trees, true tree surgeons that first assess their patient carefully, diagnosing the exact location where the feeding beetle grub is eating away at the tree's insides, and then making an incision to remove the problem. In these cultures there is a tremendous respect for woodpeckers and the role that they play within woodlands, some go as far as believing that woodpeckers can even cure sick trees by performing their surgery. But as Gorman succinctly points out in his fabulous book, *the woodpecker does not magically cure trees plagued with invertebrates: it simply dines upon the insects*.

A similar tale, also retold by Gorman, is found in the folklore of Vietnam in South East Asia; it is a tale with a moral similar to our own saying, 'pride comes before a fall'. The story describes a large proud oak that doesn't want just any bird sitting in its branches; it wants to only have pretty songbirds and doesn't want 'ugly' woodpeckers, nor does the tree want to be disturbed by woodpeckers noisily pecking away on it; so the tree tells the woodpeckers to go away and leave it in peace. The woodpeckers, patient beings, do their best to explain that they aren't in fact disturbing the tree, they are actually helping it, ridding it of harmful insect larvae that are causing it damage, but the proud tree is not prepared to listen; it is incomprehensible to the tree why it, a big and strong and mighty oak, would need the help of mere woodpeckers. To the tree, these birds are nothing more than an annoyance. The outcome of the tale is predictable. The tree, now woodpecker-free, soon becomes ill as the grubs within it grow and feed voraciously on its internal timber. The tree pleads for help from the pretty songbirds that adorn the branches, but they are unable to help it as their bills are too weak to extract the grubs. The mighty oak has to eat humble pie and beg the woodpeckers to return, and when they do they meticulously examine the tree, locating and then pulling out all the grubs they can find and curing the tree of its ills. It's a quaint moralistic story, but it is based on the ecological role of woodpeckers, portraying them as useful to trees rather than damaging to them. It is also a story that has echoes in scientific research.

The European three-toed woodpecker is a relatively small species of woodpecker, a few centimetres smaller than our own familiar great spotted. It is a bird of the spruce forests of central and northern Europe, a shy species, wary of humans, but it is one well worth seeking out. It has the typical pied plumage of many European woodpeckers, but this is accentuated by a brilliant flash of white that runs down its back from the nape to the tail. It is a truly beautiful bird to behold. The male's distinctively striped head, topped off with a yellow crown, helps to differentiate it from the other European black and white species which have much more white in the face, and red flashes on their crowns.

Britain has a real paucity of native conifer species – only three – and we have no native spruce species, but Europe has two, with the Norway spruce by far the most abundant (the other a closely related tree the Serbian spruce, its more limited distribution hinted at by its name). The three-toed woodpecker's range in Europe mirrors almost exactly the native range of the Norway spruce, which despite its name, isn't restricted to Norway. The bird and the tree go together. In Britain, our perception of spruce is heavily tainted by the dark, densely packed plantations of (mainly) Sitka spruce[27] that march across our uplands in unnatural geometric shapes. These plantations are often biological deserts in their interior, with only a handful of species to be found. But the natural spruce woodlands (usually well mixed with other tree species) of Europe are not at all like these manmade plantations; they are wonderfully vibrant places, full of life.

The Norway spruce is food for the larvae of the spruce-bark beetle, and the spruce-bark beetle larvae are the main food for the three-toed woodpecker. There are a few insect species that could be referred to as 'spruce-bark beetle', but by far the most abundant – and the one most heavily linked to the native European range of the Norway spruce and therefore to the three-toed woodpeckers – is the larger eight-toothed European spruce bark beetle (a bit of a mouthful, hence me calling it the spruce-bark beetle!).

The beetles may be small (the adults only reach about half a centimetre in length), but the damage they can wreak on stands of spruce can be extensive. They can periodically explode in number, suddenly forming large concentrations known as outbreaks. These outbreaks can be devastating for the trees, and they can also have a huge economic impact on commercial spruce plantations. As a result of the potential impact this beetle can have on commercial forestry, it is one of the few insects in Britain classified as notifiable, meaning that if you see one you must report it immediately to the plant health authorities. Since 2018, small isolated breeding populations of this beetle have been discovered in south-east England, but in 2021 a large number of new outbreaks were found across Kent and East Sussex, suggesting that the beetles were spreading. In response, statutory felling notices have been issued, but it remains to be seen whether these will curtail the spread of this small beetle.

Within its natural range of central and northern Europe, there have been many studies looking at how the populations of this beetle are regulated in natural conditions, and how their numbers are kept in check by natural processes. In the past, vertebrate predators such as birds were thought to have little impact on numbers of these beetles, playing only a trivial role in the population dynamics of these spruce-consuming insects. However, in 2005 a study by Philippe Fayt, Marlene Machmer and Christoph Steeger[28] reversed that perception, their paper strongly suggesting that the three-toed woodpecker in fact plays a significant role in regulating bark beetle populations in coniferous forest landscapes, and that when an outbreak occurs the birds can respond rapidly and play a stabilising role in

---

27 A species that comes from the Pacific seaboard of North America. It was first introduced to Britain in 1831 and is now one of the main forestry species grown here.

28 The paper, 'Regulation of spruce bark beetles by woodpeckers – a literature review', is widely available on the internet.

the population dynamics of the beetle. In other words, the three-toed woodpecker helps keep the beetle population in check. By digging into the spruce to winkle out the beetle larvae, the bird isn't damaging the tree, it's helping it – and its neighbours and its neighbour's neighbours. The woodpecker is removing the beetles before they can develop into adults, preventing them dispersing and breeding and doing further damage to other spruce trees in the vicinity. The birds are stopping the outbreak from breaking out. The woodpecker and its tree-pecking feeding technique does indeed cause superficial damage to the tree, but importantly it is protecting them in the longer term.

The three-toed woodpecker, then, the natural regulator of this spruce-bark beetle, is a key player in the natural balance of the European spruce forest ecosystem. Nature is amazing at regulating itself, but there is something more amazing in this relationship between the tree, the beetle and the bird, something that at first we may not notice, but when we look a bit harder becomes apparent. When numbers of the tree-consuming beetles build up in an area, the woodpeckers are somehow able to detect this sudden abundance and they will then move, sometimes considerable distances, into the affected areas.

Once again, though, humans are creating problems. The bird's ability to move large distances to find the increased numbers of beetles is strongly linked to the structure of the larger landscape, and as this gets increasingly fragmented by our own activities, as the extent of contiguous woodland is reduced, the ability for the woodpeckers to perform their ecological role becomes more and more reduced, leading to the beetle becoming increasingly unregulated and unchecked in its behaviour, which in turn leads to more economically damaging outbreaks.

But just how do the birds know that there is a build-up of beetle grubs in the first place? How do they know to suddenly up sticks from where they are and move considerable distances to exploit this food resource? As yet nobody knows for sure, but we can make educated guesses. Remember how the oak tree in the Vietnamese story asked the woodpecker to come and help it? It might not be as farfetched as it sounds …

Trees communicate with each other – they 'talk' to one another. But they don't use sound as we do; they use the language of scent.[29] At first glance, the thought that something communicates by scent seems odd to us, but in fact we do it ourselves; it is just that we don't realise that we do. There is plenty of scientific evidence that suggests that scented chemical compounds, called pheromones, play a big part in how we choose our long-term partners. If you are still doubtful about communication by scent, watch what your dog does when it goes past a lamp-post.

One of the major 'talking points' for trees is the fact that they are constantly under attack by creatures wanting to eat their leaves. Trees produce their leaves for photosynthesis, not

---

29 They are also able to communicate via their root systems, which are plugged into one another by the mycorrhizal fungal networks that form the woodwide web I mentioned briefly earlier. Trees are talkers – if only all of us would listen!

for an animal or insect to eat, and they will do many things to combat anything that tries to do so. Spines are an obvious defence against browsing animals. In Britain the holly is a good example; it produces sharp needle-like spines on its leaves to deter mammalian grazers, but as the tree grows taller so that its leaves are out of reach of deer and the like, or if the browsing pressure is reduced, the leaves of the tree slowly[30] revert to type, becoming simple oval shapes. Holly leaves are spiny only in order to protect them from the deleterious effect of browsing. The browsers that hollies have to contend with in Britain are relatively short in their reach, but the trees that grow on the African savannah have to contend with the tallest browsers of all, giraffes.

The characteristic trees of those African grasslands, the iconic shapes that adorn many a tourist image, are the acacias. Except they are not. Unfortunately, a change in taxonomy in 2009 now means that they are no longer called acacias. Biologically speaking, they are now known as vachellias instead, and the name 'acacia' is now officially used for the species that are native to Australia and New Zealand – yet another example of our continuous quest for order in the world we see. Unsurprisingly this name change hasn't caught on, and the African trees are still widely called acacias. One of these no-longer-acacia trees is the impressively named umbrella thorn, and it was whilst watching giraffes browsing on a group of these trees that researchers discovered that the trees were communicating with one another.

Despite the fiercely protective thorns that these trees possess, the giraffes are able to browse on their leaves, but as soon as they start to munch the leaves, the tree being fed on reacts by creating bitter-tasting compounds to flood its leaves with, making them unpalatable to the giraffes. But this chemical defence takes a few minutes to kick in – as we have seen, trees are slow beasts – so the giraffes can continue to browse for a short time before their food becomes too distasteful for them to stomach. Then the giraffes move on to other trees, to continue their feeding. But the researchers observing them noticed that they didn't just go to the next tree to feed, but to trees that were considerable distances away. It became apparent that the trees growing within about 100 metres of the first one knew what was coming and had already filled their leaves with the distasteful compounds in anticipation of the attack. The giraffes – from bitter experience you could say – knowing that this was the case didn't waste their time attempting to browse the neighbouring trees.

Further research followed, and this has shown that when one of the umbrella thorns starts to be browsed, it doesn't just produce chemicals to flood its own leaves with, but it produces other chemicals and releases them into the air to warn nearby trees that they too are in danger of being browsed. These other trees detect this distress scent and begin the process of producing their own noxious-tasting compounds to flood its leaves with.

---

30 The individual leaves aren't capable of changing shape of course; it is as the tree renews them that the change occurs. But holly leaves are much more persistent than leaves on deciduous trees; holly leaves can be present on a tree for five years, meaning that any response to grazing pressure is a very slow one. This can lead to us misinterpreting what the tree's leaves mean.

There has been much more research on this topic, and it turns out that these no-longer-acacias are not unique in doing this, and that many, many members of the plant kingdom release these warning pheromones when they are under attack. Sometimes this messaging is something that we can detect, even if we don't understand what we are detecting. When you or your neighbour cut the grass, that beautiful aroma you smell as the mower mows – that smell so reminiscent of British summertime – is actually a chemical warning to other grasses in the area that a browser is active. Unfortunately for the insects and other wildlife that would abound in grasslands if only they weren't so manicured, grass hasn't yet evolved a chemical compound that can put off a mower.

But trees aren't satisfied with just talking to each other. Other studies, relating to trees as diverse and completely unrelated to one another as elms and pines, have shown that as soon as they detect the presence of an adult invertebrate whose young feed on their leaves, they can release a chemical signal to attract specific parasitoid wasps that lay their own eggs in the eggs of the invertebrate species that feed on the tree. The trees are undertaking a deliberate action to attract these wasps. They are actually calling for pest control – and what's more, they already know the number! That is absolutely amazing! The trees have evolved the ability to not just recognise a specific threat, but also to contact another organism that actually controls that specific threat. It is a mind-blowing cry for help. But does this cry-for-help tactic involve birds as well?

This is where it can start to get a bit tricky. It has been suggested that our two native oak species, the pedunculate and the sessile, signal chemically to blue tits when they are under attack from defoliating caterpillars, and that the birds respond to these signals and home in on the tree to feed on the caterpillars. It is estimated that a single blue tit can eat around 100 of these caterpillars a day, and when the birds have young to feed, the numbers they can pluck off the leaves of the oaks can get very large indeed.[31] Even though the idea would be amazing for us, it would make sense if the trees were able to intentionally call in the birds – but are they really doing this? Instead of deliberately attracting the birds, are the oaks in fact only doing what the umbrella thorns do in Africa – that is, releasing pheromones to warn other nearby trees that they too could be attacked? Has the wily blue tit learnt that this pheromone signal means food for them?

Other studies have already shown that blue tits can detect pheromones that aren't intended for them. For example, the winter moth is an abundant moth species of northern and central Europe; unusually, the female winter moth doesn't have any wings so, being flightless, she can't go looking for a mate when she wants her eggs fertilised. So she calls for one. She will climb up a plant or tree stem, gaining a bit of height to help broadcast her message, and once high enough releases pheromones that are wafted along in the air currents. But the blue tit, as well as other insectivorous bird species, has learnt to intercept

---

31 It has been estimated that for a typical small passerine as many as 6,000 caterpillars are needed to successfully raise a brood of four chicks.

these chemical love letters, and uses them to locate the female moth (packed full of protein) which it then eats.

The birds are listening in on the insect's communications – or, if you like, the birds are bugging the bug. Blue tits are clever birds; they are very good at learning, especially where food is concerned – after all, back in the day, they soon learnt to peck through the silver foil tops of milk bottles so that they could feed on the cream within. The winter moth obviously isn't trying to communicate with the blue tit – that would be suicidal – but the bird has learnt that the chemical signal it detects comes from a source of food. The big question is: has it done similar with the oaks? Is it just picking up on their intraspecific chatter and taking advantage of it, or are the trees actively signalling to the bird?

With that in mind, let's return to the question of what's happening with the spruce, the woodpecker and the spruce-bark beetle. It seems highly likely to me that there is some sort of chemical signalling going on, and that the woodpeckers are responding to it. But who's signalling to whom, and why? Those beetles, like many invertebrates, use pheromones in their breeding strategy, and this is used against them by us humans in pheromone-laced traps, as part of the control methods in commercial forestry plantations. Could it be that the woodpeckers are, just like the tits with the moths, intercepting these messages and using them to locate the larvae on which they feed? But we also know that tree species release pheromones to warn other trees that they are under attack. Is this what the Norway spruce are doing? Are they 'talking' to one another, warning their fellows of an imminent beetle outbreak? Is the woodpecker eavesdropping on that communication – has it learnt that that communication signifies abundant food for it? Or are the trees deliberately calling for help from the woodpeckers, as in that story about the oak in Vietnam? After all, as mentioned earlier, it has been shown that pines, a close relative of the spruces, do something similar with parasitoid wasps.

Told you it would get tricky. This hidden world of communication is one we have only recently discovered, and personally I think it is going to take quite a while to unravel exactly what's going on. We humans might have thought we'd mastered communications – but all we can do is talk to other humans, and even then not everyone understands. We are only now beginning to realise that we have been shut out of a whole world of chatter we never even knew was going on.

Before we leave the woodpeckers behind, I want to take you back to the species I encountered so often in my forestry days, the great spotted. These thrush-sized birds are doing well in Britain; unlike so many species they are actually expanding their range and have now even colonised the Republic of Ireland. They can be found throughout the British Isles and, to the delight of many, are becoming an increasingly common garden bird as well. They have learnt that our bird feeders are a good source of food for them, particularly fat balls and peanuts, and it could well be that their increase in population and range is being fuelled by this fuel we put out.

Their visit to gardens has meant that these attractive birds have become much more familiar to a wider human audience, and it is not just their black and white[32] plumage that has become familiar, but so too has their song. Except it isn't a song in the traditional sense of the word; instead of using their vocal chords they use percussion.

Other than a loud and crisp call often given as they fly overhead, the great spotted is a largely silent woodpecker when it comes to vocalisations, but it does still announce itself to potential mates and rivals every year with its drumming. For me, a drumming woodpecker is a sure sign that spring is finally on its way after the short days and cold weather of winter; it's a sound that you can hear from late January and early February, the males staking their claim to the territory with a bit of head banging!

To make its drumming the great spotted woodpecker strikes its bill hard and rapidly against a tree trunk or branch, a roll of percussive sound so fast it is impossible to discern how many individual bangs there are within it.[33] Once the birds have paired up, the drumming reduces right down, but if a male is unlucky in love he will continue the percussion; some have been recorded performing up to 400 drum rolls a day in their unanswered quest for a mate. An avian equivalent of banging your head against a brick wall.

Banging your head against anything is not to be recommended, be you human or bird, but woodpeckers are no ordinary birds. The impact force of a great spotted woodpecker drumming has been measured at around 1,000 times that of gravity, or about 1,000 g. To put that into perspective, if we suffered a 100g bang to our heads we would die, but these small birds, no bigger than a blackbird, can take ten times that force. These are birds that have evolved to drum. Woodpeckers such as the great spotted have some adaptations that act to absorb the shock generated by drumming; some of the bones that make up the skull have an almost sponge-like structure to them, allowing the bones to absorb and dissipate the force of the impact.[34] They also have an additional bone structure that no other birds have, which helps secure the brain casing, stopping the otherwise damaging concussive movements of the brain that would occur as the bill is impacted against the wood.

And then there is the wood itself. The great spotted woodpecker that you hear serenading the arrival of spring isn't drumming against solid timber; it does its drumming against hollow dead wood. This helps lessen the impact caused by the drumming, but it also ensures that the sound reverberates far and wide, and that is exactly what the woodpecker requires. The bird selects its drumming post with care and will use it for encore after encore, returning to it to perform as required. Dead wood occurs naturally in trees, as we have seen, and the bird uses it to communicate with other woodpeckers in what could be described as a trunk call.[35]

---

32 They also have a red vent on the underside, and the males have a red patch on the rear of their heads.

33 It is estimated that they make 10 to 16 strikes per second.

34 This bone structure has been copied by us humans in the construction of crash helmets.

35 Apologies.

The use of dead and hollow parts of a tree to drum on is of course a form of commensalism. The tree neither gets any benefit nor suffers any harm as a result of the bird's actions, whilst the woodpecker benefits greatly from the acoustic effects of the wood. It is yet another example of a relationship between birds and trees – but it is a relationship threatened by our obsession with tidiness. Woodpeckers need dead wood to nest in and to drum on, and by removing dead wood unnecessarily from woodlands we are also removing vital components of the bird's habitat. Safety rightly plays a part in our management of dead wood, but more often than not dead wood is removed from a tree's canopy unnecessarily. Dead wood is an important habitat, and many of our red-listed beetles, for example, depend on it – but it is also the source of one of the most evocative sounds in nature, and we should never silence these drums.

Spring cleaning

Leaving woodpeckers, their drumming and the general intrigue of tree communications behind, we will now undertake a diversion into the nesting habits of some raptor species. Raptors, or birds of prey, typically make a platform nest in trees, a cupped arrangement of twigs and branches. In my years as a forest ranger I had the privilege of working alongside the goshawk, a very raptorious raptor indeed. Goshawks are native to Britain. They are meant to be here, to be part of our woodland ecosystems. Sadly, though, the ignorance of humans can be very destructive, especially when it comes to the vested interest of rearing game to kill for fun. Goshawks, like so many of our predatory species – be they mammalian or avian – have been subject to unrelenting persecution by shooting estates primarily interested in maximising the number of game birds they can produce to be shot. This persecution reached its zenith in the late Victorian and Edwardian eras. The killing was too much for the goshawk, and it was driven to extinction in Britain during the late 19th century.

But the bird has returned, and has become re-established in many parts of the country. Its numbers are increasing, and it's regaining its place as a top predator in many of our natural ecosystems, even though by its very nature it is still a hard bird for many birders to connect with. When I was a ranger one of the most frequent questions I would get asked was 'Where can I see a goshawk?' Unfortunately it was a question I was always vague about answering. They might have made a strong comeback, but sadly this magnificent bird of prey is still deliberately persecuted by criminals who feel they have the right to illegally deprive of us of its presence. During the last century the vast majority of people in this country rejected the Victorian attitudes to wildlife; sadly, though, there are still a small minority of small-minded people, particularly in the game bird-rearing industry, that didn't. Raptor persecution is very much ongoing in modern-day Britain, and it's a shameful stain on our society.[36]

---

36 It may be a small number of people, but raptor persecution in the UK is widespread and persistent. To get an idea of how bad it is, see the excellent blog site of Raptor Persecution UK, www.raptorpersecutionscotland.wordpress.com. It's an often sad and infuriating read, but a must.

You may be able to tell that the continued criminal activity of killing our raptors annoys me! I'm not the only one to be annoyed by it, but I will leave it there and get back to what I was saying.

Goshawks are large members of the hawk family, resembling the more familiar but smaller sparrowhawk. I once heard a goshawk described as being a sparrowhawk on steroids – quite a good description. They are powerful birds, and if you are ever lucky enough to get a good sustained view of one you will see where that analogy comes from. They are much bulkier birds than their smaller relative, and they exude power. Goshawks build a large, cupped, platform nest in trees, typically situated on a branch junction alongside the trunk at the bottom of the canopy. This is a good location, for these are big birds that can carry large prey items, so they need easy flight access to the nest, but they also require the cover the surrounding canopy affords them. As with many birds of prey, the nests can be reused in successive years, the structure getting bigger each year as more material is added to it. In Britain, the birds start laying their eggs at the beginning of April, so late February and into March is the main time for nest building or renovation. By the time the large female[37] settles down on the nest, the flow of new material being brought in will have stopped.

Goshawks average between three and four chicks in the nest – although I monitored one nest that successfully fledged five – and as the goshawk chicks grow, they are fed with a constant succession of prey items. The chicks are in the nest for around five to six weeks before they fledge. When they are very young, the adults will bring the prey item to the nest, and using their tremendous talons and fearsome beak, will tear it up into small parcels and feed the chicks themselves. Once the chicks are sated, the remains of the prey item are often left on the nest for the young chicks to peck curiously at. As the chicks get older, feeding time on the nest can get a bit hectic, to say the least, as the chicks fight amongst themselves over who gets the choicest morsels. At this stage, the adult birds tend to fly in, drop the prey item into the nest and then fly off again to avoid getting entangled in the scrum of pin feathers, sharp talons and grasping bills. The adult birds are skilled hunters, killing a wide range of prey items and supplying the chicks with them. There is usually an excess of prey, and the chicks can often be seen idly pecking at food remains on the nest when they are not actually hungry.

When I was in the forests and trying to locate the nests of these brilliant birds so that they could be monitored and protected, I would look for a number of clues. The birds themselves are notoriously difficult to get to grips with – their nickname 'phantoms of the forest' is a very good one – so it was signs of the birds you would look for rather than the birds themselves. Once I had narrowed down my search area by interpreting the clues on the forest floor, I would begin to look up into the trees to try and locate potential nest structures. Platforms of sticks in the dark lower canopy of conifers can be tricky to find, yet they can also be surprisingly numerous. Goshawks' nesting behaviour varies; some will stick to using

---

37 Goshawks exhibit sexual dimorphism; the females are significantly bigger than the males.

Illegally poisoned goshawks, the much bigger female on the left.

just one nest year after year, others will build new ones each time they breed; and some will have three or four platforms and alternate between them.

These nests can be quite large, and when looking up from the ground some distance away it can often be impossible to actually see any activity in or on the nest itself. But one of the giveaways I used to look out for once the chicks had hatched[38] was the addition of fresh new material to the nest platform – not sticks and old twigs, but fresh sprigs of conifer shoots, replete with an abundance of green needles. The adults would start bringing this new material into the nest as soon as the chicks were a few days old, and they would continue until the chicks were at the branching stage.[39]

---

38 Once chicks have hatched the adult activity around the nest increases. It is at this stage that the birds become a bit more noticeable, and it was usually at this stage that I would be dispatched to investigate a potential site. Also, once the chicks have hatched, the risk of desertion by the adults significantly reduces, meaning that it is far better to monitor sites after the eggs have hatched. All monitoring of goshawk requires licensing.

39 The branching stage is when the chicks are able to move about the branches of the tree the nest is located in. They are still very much tied to the nest, but during the day they are beginning to explore a bit more.

The addition of this material doesn't offer anything structurally, and the idea of a goshawk wanting to camouflage its nest[40] doesn't make a lot of sense, in that virtually anything with any nous gives the nest of the goshawk a wide berth. Chris Packham's moniker for them, 'avian terminators', is a good one! To collect this fresh green material, the adults can't just pick it up off the forest floor as they would the twigs and sticks they'd constructed the nest itself with; they would have to physically pick the small branches from the trees, using their fearsome bills as secateurs. This is not easy for a big bird to do – it's something that takes effort and dexterity to achieve – and whatever the reason for the bird exhibiting this behaviour, it certainly isn't something that is done frivolously. It is done with purpose.

When I was monitoring the birds, I was intrigued by this behaviour. I also used to find it very helpful in pinpointing the actual site of a live nest – but I wasn't sure of its purpose. One thing that I did notice, however, was that the adult birds in my area would invariably select the green needle-strewn branches of Douglas fir to bring into their nest of chicks. While Douglas fir is a popular timber tree in many parts of Britain, and it was plentiful in the forests I worked in, I noticed that this tree seemed to be the one they would choose even when the nest was located in stands of other species, including Norway spruce and Scots pine, and even in (only rarely) deciduous trees.

It should be said that I have a soft spot for the Douglas fir. They're beautiful trees, elegant giants that tower away upwards. Again, as with spruce, our image of them in Britain is tainted by past forestry practices – dark gloomy forests laid out in grids – but we should see beyond that and look at the tree itself. We mustn't ever forget that the way we have chosen to use the tree is not its fault. Britain's tallest tree is a still relatively young Douglas fir, and it is extremely likely that if we humans hadn't felled the old growth forests on the North American Pacific seaboard in which they are native, they would be the tallest trees in the world. They certainly would dwarf the current tallest trees in the world.[41] The bright green needles of the Douglas are soft and very fragrant; crush them in your hand and you get a powerful blast of a clean citrus/pine odour, a smell that always takes me back to my childhood, when my mum would swab the decks of the kitchen floor with a similar-smelling disinfectant.

And that memory, recalled by the crushed foliage of the tree, could well be the reason that the goshawk adorns its nest with these branches.

It is no coincidence that many household disinfectants smell like crushed conifer foliage; the volatile aromatic terpene compounds produced by many species of conifer are used

---

40 It has been previously suggested that the addition of fresh green material to active nests could be an attempt to try and camouflage them; conversely others have suggested that it is a mechanism for advertising them, a way of showing to other birds of the same species that the nest and the territory is very much occupied.

41 The tallest trees in the world currently are the coast redwoods, but they are only so because we haven't felled them. But we did fell the tall Douglas firs of the area (their timber is valued above that of the redwood); some of those Douglas firs were at least 30 metres taller than the tallest coast redwoods.

in many of those products. These chemicals are very effective at killing a wide variety of bacterial and fungal pathogens, including bacteria of the streptococcus and staphylococcus genera. These bacteria are naturally found in wild bird populations, especially in faecal matter; normally their effects are mild, but when birds are concentrated health problems can and do occur.

Birds in a nest are concentrated – they can't be anything else – and they obviously defecate, meaning that they are concentrated with the medium that potentially carries these bacterial pathogens. As the chicks grow, they are able to make their way to the edge of the nest where they can squirt their faeces overboard by several metres (which is very impressive to see, as long as you're out of the firing line), but initially they are unable to do this, and faecal build-up in the nest is inevitable. But it is not just bacteria in faecal matter that can be an issue; the nests of birds of prey also contain plenty of prey remains – bits of rotting meat and digestive tracts – items that can attract a whole host of invertebrates that could threaten the health of young chicks. So the potential for the nest to become an unhealthy environment for the chicks is high. Could it be that the goshawks that I witnessed bringing in green conifer material to their nests were doing so to disinfect and clean them? An example of a bird building a nest in one tree, then using material from another tree to maintain that nest's hygiene?

Raptors aren't the only birds that will add fresh green material after the original construction of their nest; male starlings will add fresh green material to the nest prior to egg laying, in what is believed to be an attempt to impress potential mates. But the raptors that exhibit this behaviour – and not all species do – add the material only once the chicks have hatched, so this behaviour can have nothing to do with impressing a mate.

An old goshawk nest, showing the bones of prey items.

It has been shown in studies that the birds bring more fresh green material to the nest in the first half of the nestling period, the amount dropping in the second half as the chicks get bigger. From the hygiene point of view this makes sense. As mentioned above, when the chicks are young they defecate within the nest, so if there was a time to disinfect the nest it would surely be in this period. As the chicks get bigger they become much more mobile in the nest, enabling them to defecate over the nest's sides, so the reduction in adding fresh green material at this stage fits well with the theory.

It has to be said, though, that not everyone agrees with this theory, and it is a difficult one to substantiate, but increasingly studies are showing a link between the behaviour of adding green nest material and its benefits to nest hygiene. In 2013 one highly respected American biologist and author, Bernd Heinrich, published a paper on this subject;[42] in it he reviews the possible explanations for the addition of fresh green material at the nestling stage, and concludes that nest hygiene is by far the most plausible explanation for the behaviour.

Another American study[43] looked at the nesting behaviour of the red-shouldered hawk (a close relative of our own common buzzard), a widespread breeder in the eastern half of the United States. This study showed that the birds selected foliage from certain tree species to add to the nest at frequencies higher than expected. The main species selected wasn't a conifer, but the black cherry, and its leafy material was found in over 80 per cent of the 63 nests they studied, despite the fact that the tree only made up 4 to 5 per cent of the trees in the forest area in which the nests were located. Black cherry, like many members of the *Prunus* genus,[44] has cyanide compounds in its tissues, but this species in particular is noted for high concentrations of those compounds throughout the tree. As its leaves wilt the cyanide compounds increase; in other words, once the leaves are picked, or plucked, they produce more cyanide. This study suggests that the birds are deliberately seeking out that species of tree. Once the hawks have identified a black cherry tree (birds identifying trees to species level!), they collect from it small branches covered in foliage before taking these back to their nests, where they incorporate them into the existing structure as a lining – a lining that as it wilts and dries out releases cyanide compounds that kill the invertebrates within the structure of the nest. The hawks are fumigating their nests.

---

42 The article, 'Why does a Hawk Build with Green Nesting Material?', was published in the peer-reviewed *Northeastern Naturalist Journal* vol 20, no.2.

43 The study, 'Selection of Fresh Vegetation for Nest Lining by Red-shouldered Hawks' by Cheryl R. Dykstra et al, was published in 2009 in the peer-reviewed *Wilson Journal of Ornithology*, issue 121.

44 A genus that contains British natives such as wild cherry and blackthorn as well as species such as peach and apricot.

The Bonelli's eagle is a beautiful bird that I have had many close encounters with in Extremadura, a place where I spend as much time as I can. They are powerful hunters, taking both avian and mammalian prey, using their utterly fearsome and proportionally huge killing talon[45] to dispatch whatever they catch. Another study looked at this species and its nesting habits in Spain;[46] this piece of research demonstrated that these highly territorial (and somewhat aggressive) birds would use fresh green material from the maritime pine trees that grew within their territory to add to the nest once the chicks had hatched – that is, long after the nest construction had been completed. Maritime pine is noted for high concentrates of aromatic compounds that are particularly repellent to insects, something that would be useful in a nest in a warm climate with an accumulation of animal prey remains within it! This study compared the breeding success of eagles that had no maritime pine growing in their territory with that of eagles that were able to access and use this green material. The results showed that nests with maritime pine in them had a lower presence of ectoparasites – particularly ones such as blowfly larvae, maggots, that could potentially harm young chicks – than those that had none, and that the nests with pine needle material present also had correspondingly higher breeding success. Blowfly larvae feed on flesh, and if you think about how the downy bodies of the eagle's young chicks are going to be pressed up against the food remains in the nest that the flies are laying their eggs on, it becomes easy to see how their presence could cause serious impact to the very young and vulnerable chicks. Bonelli's eagles are fearsome defenders of their nest sites and their young; on several memorable occasions I have watched them attack and drive off (much bigger) golden eagles that had strayed too close to the nest and the precious chicks within. Against these large predators the Bonellis use their aggression, but against the much smaller invertebrate predators it would appear that they use their nous.

It seems, then, as if 'pine fresh' isn't just an important marketing slogan for floor cleaners. Although there is an argument against this point of view, scientific research is increasingly showing a link between the use of fresh green material at the nestling stage and nest hygiene in raptors. Personally, I think that this link is very real. Thinking back to my time in the forests with goshawks, I can't come up with an alternative explanation that fits; goshawk chicks are going to be just as vulnerable to maggots as Bonelli's eagle chicks, and it makes sense to me that a bird that will readily defend the nest from larger species is also going to try and defend it from much smaller ones. Nature is always purposeful in what it does, and the only logical purpose that I can come up with for this behaviour is the one that is being increasingly backed up by scientific research.

---

45 The hallux, back claw, on each foot.

46 Entitled 'Green plant material versus ectoparasites in nests of Bonelli's eagle' by Diego Ontiveros et al; it was published in 2007 in the peer-reviewed *Journal of Zoology*.

While scientific research is by its very nature unemotional in its very matter-of-fact conclusions, that doesn't mean we should forget just how incredible this behaviour is. These are birds that it would seem are deliberately selecting material from specific trees in the apparent knowledge that this particular material will convey on them an advantage when it comes to successfully raising their chicks. That is something that raises so many questions – not least: How do birds identify individual species of tree? Could *you* identify a black cherry tree or a maritime pine tree without the help of a field guide? In my opinion, what these birds are doing is quite simply remarkable.

Bonelli's eagle

Part Three
Mutual friends

Mutual friends

Mutually beneficial

So far we have looked at relatively simple relationships between the trees and the birds, relationships that tend to favour the birds, be that through the trees providing a launch pad, a place to perch, a place to store, kill or process food, or a place to nest, or even by providing a method to help keep those nests clean. But in amongst these basic relationships we have touched on potentially more complicated ones. For example, just how are those woodpeckers discovering the build-ups of spruce-damaging larvae? It could be that the relationship between the three-toed woodpecker of central Europe and the Norway spruce trees that grow in its forests is a mutually beneficial one, a relationship that has evolved over time, in which the bird gets a benefit from the tree somehow signalling to it that there is a build-up of food present and the tree gets the benefit, although tempered by the chiselling required, of the bird removing the insects within its tissues and interrupting the breeding cycle of the beetle.

Not all symbiotic mutually beneficial relationships between trees and birds are obvious, and there is no doubt that there are many, many more awaiting our discovery. However, there are some relationships between the two that are not just mutually beneficial but are also easily recognised by us humans as being so. These are relationships related to the reproduction of the trees, be that how they reproduce in the first place or how they then ensure that the resulting progeny get the best start in life.

Let's start at the beginning of the reproductive process and introduce a word that was new to me before I started writing this book. It is a wonderful word.

Ornithophily

The vast majority of flowering plants, including of course the trees, need their flowers to be pollinated so that they can set seed and produce future plants (and trees). There are many mechanisms in place for this, including self-pollination and wind pollination and, perhaps the best known, insect pollination, or entomophily. If you ask someone how a plant is pollinated they will inevitably think of bees; but it's not just bees that pollinate flowers, and indeed it's not just insects; birds too are pollinators. The birds and the bees indeed.

The process of bird pollination is known as ornithophily, it's something that we don't normally think of as occurring in Britain, associating it with more tropical climes, and we're right to do so. Most known examples of ornithophily do indeed occur in the tropics, as well as in southern Africa and on several island chains – generally places far warmer than our own country. The group of birds that we most associate with this process are of course the hummingbirds, arguably some of the most amazing bird species on the planet. The blurred whirring wings of these remarkable little flyers are incredible to witness as they position themselves perfectly in three-dimensional space. They can manoeuvre themselves in any direction – up, down, sideways, diagonally and even backwards – the flight skills of the hummingbirds are something that aeronautical engineers can only dream about.

A bird that I dream about seeing is one of these; it is a birding jewel, an endemic of the island of Cuba and found nowhere else on Earth. The bee hummingbird, an appropriately named species, is so tiny that it makes our familiar house sparrow look like a giant. The male bee hummingbird measures just 5½ centimetres long, including its proportionally long bill. I've watched plenty of footage of these dazzling flyers in action, and they do indeed look more insect-like than bird-like as they buzz between flowers, feeding on the nectar within and pollinating them at the same time.

Although they may be tiny in size, they are not in appetite; bee hummingbirds are prolific feeders. But then they have to be. It has been estimated that a single bird can feed from as many as 1,500 flowers in a single day, and the calorie burn needed to fuel the ferociously fast wing beats (they have been recorded as beating their wings at an extraordinary 80 times a second!) means that these birds constantly have to top up on the sugar-rich nectar (the original biofuel) that the flowers offer as their incentive. The species of trees that this, the world's smallest bird, visits have coevolved with these avian pollinators; their flowers are deliberately coloured red as an arboreal signal to attract the birds. These red flowers provide the nectar that the hummingbird has to imbibe to survive, and their shape enables the bird to access that nectar easily.

That deliberate shaping of the flower, honed by millennia of co-evolution, also ensures that the tree too gets what it wants. Because as the bee hummingbird plunges its relatively long bill (size is most definitely relative when the bird is this small!) deep into the flower's structure, it cannot avoid picking up liberal amounts of the flower's pollen not only on its bill but also on its forehead. This is the purpose of the flower's structure; to ensure the maximum chance of its pollen being deposited onto the bird. The bird then rapidly transports the pollen to other nearby flowers and so pollination happens, the tree's flowers are fertilised, the seed is set and the next generation of trees can begin their journey. The hummingbird, of course, gets the food it needs to not only survive but also to breed and rear its very own next generation of miniature avian delights. It is a perfect example of a mutually symbiotic relationship, a win-win for both parties.

The trees that the bee hummingbirds feed upon and pollinate include species such as the wild tamarind, a member of the pea family related to the acacias, and which can grow to a height of 20 metres or more. It is also an important pollinator of smaller, scrubbier trees in the coffee family, a huge group of plants found mainly in the tropics. One of the plants in this family has the colloquial name of hummingbird bush because of its association with these flying marvels. This small tree is often planted in gardens in Florida to attract other species of hummingbird, which also feed on the specially evolved flowers. Let's face it; if you could attract hummingbirds to your garden by planting a small scrubby tree, you would!

There are around 360 species of hummingbird scattered across the Americas, found as breeding birds from Tierra del Fuego right up to Alaska, although the vast majority of the species are much more tropical in their distribution. All of them are nectarivorous, although they will also eat the odd invertebrate. Hummingbirds feed from, and pollinate, the flowers of everything from small plants right through to tall trees. The birds have coevolved with the plants, and the differing bill shapes of the hummingbird species correlate with the shape of the flowers that they mainly feed upon. Most hummingbird species specialise on feeding on a small variety of flowering species and not all of them feed on tree flowers, but those that do perform a vital role in the ecology of those tree species.

There are more bird families that are important pollinators of flowers. In Africa and parts of Asia sunbirds are vital pollinators of many species, including several trees. There are around 145 species of sunbird, most of which feed on nectar, although one group, the spider hunters, supplement this diet with a specialism for arachnids. Sunbirds can be just as beautiful as hummingbirds, the male golden-winged sunbird living up to its name in the breeding season, its dazzling wings glinting metallically in the sunshine. This bird is one of several sunbirds that feed on the nectar of numerous species of African coral trees in the *Erythrina* genus of the pea family,[47] and as these birds feed on the nectar they pollinate the flowers, much as the hummingbirds do. The common name of the species of trees principally pollinated by sunbirds indicates the colour of their flowers, which are in the red spectrum. Whilst the feeding preferences of the sunbirds is similar to those of the hummingbirds, they aren't as small or as aerially acrobatic, in that their hovering ability is limited, or even non-existent in some species, potentially restricting their access to the flowers. However, the trees have evolved to counteract that problem, their flowers blooming in locations easily reachable from other branches. So the coral trees have taken the mutually symbiotic relationship a bit further than most; they provide perches for their pollinators.

Remote island archipelagos often provide perfect conditions for unique ecological relationships to evolve, but unfortunately these relationships and the species that form

---

47 The pea family is vast and includes many tree species, some of which, like the laburnum, are commonly found in UK gardens.

them are highly vulnerable to human-induced extinction. Every time we have blundered into an ecosystem that has evolved for millennia upon millennia without the presence of large mammals such as ourselves, that intrusion has inevitably led to ecological disaster. Probably the most famous example of this happening is the dodo of the once humanless islands of Mauritius in the Indian Ocean; more on that flightless pigeon in a later chapter. The sad truth is that we don't know how many plant and animal species have become extinct on remote island chains thanks to our colonisation of them, and we really haven't a clue about how many unique symbiotic relationships have also been lost as a result.

As a sad example, the 137 volcanic islands that make up the archipelago of Hawaii in the Pacific have seen plenty of human-induced extinctions of species, along with devastation of the highly evolved ecosystems that had previously flourished on these islands. The islands of Hawaii have their own unique suite of bird pollinators. They don't have hummingbirds or sunbirds, but Hawaiian honeycreepers, a group of closely related endemic birds that are members of the finch family, the same family that our familiar chaffinch belongs to. Honeycreepers would have begun as a single species, which somehow found itself isolated on these remote islands, and then, through a process known as adaptive radiation, will have slowly evolved into a whole host of different species, each one filling a particular niche that was vacant and available on the unique isolated island environments that the particular birds found themselves in.

But Hawaiian honeycreepers have not fared well since humans first colonised the islands in the early 13th century. It is widely thought that back then there were around 57 unique species of these highly specialised birds; now there are just 17, and many of these are endangered. So around 70 per cent of all the world's honeycreepers have been wiped out in just a few hundred years. The Hawaiian honeycreepers have evolved many different lifestyles and many different diets; some have become insect feeders, whilst others have specialised in snails, some seeds and others of course nectar, coevolving with the plants that feed them in much the same way as the hummingbirds and the sunbirds have done elsewhere.

The crested honeycreeper, which has the wonderfully alternative Hawaiian name of 'ākohekohe, sports a fantastic punk rock-style head crest; unfortunately, though, this is a bird that is listed as critically endangered by the IUCN.[48] It is one of the nectarivorous honeycreeper species that feed on the nectar of an endemic tree called 'ōhi'a lehua – a tree that has the unusual distinction of a scientific name, *Metrosideros polymorpha*, that is far easier for us to pronounce than its common name! As the second part[49] of the tree's scientific name would suggest, this is a tree that is highly variable in shape; indeed, it is a classic example of how confusing it can be to designate a plant as a tree.

It is a member of the myrtle family, a family that is represented in Britain by just one

---

[48] The International Union for Conservation of Nature.

[49] The first part of the (Greek-derived) name means 'iron heartwood'.

species, the more shrub-like than tree-like bog myrtle. On wet ground, this Hawaiian tree takes the form of a prostrate ground-hugging low bush, just a few centimetres high, but on drier soils it becomes a wonderful towering tree of up to 25 metres or more. Whatever form it takes though, 'ōhi'a lehua still needs to have its flowers, which are of course red, pollinated so that it can produce fertile seed. It achieves this via the honeycreepers. As well as the crested honeycreeper, another two Hawaiian honeycreeper species, the scarlet honeycreeper and 'apapane, are the main pollinators of the tree's flowers. These birds also supplement their nectar diet with fruit and insects, but are principally dependent on the tree for their food, whilst the tree is dependent on what's left of the native honeycreeper populations for its ability to produce fertile seed and therefore future trees for future birds to feed on. The Hawaiian honeycreepers and the 'ōhi'a lehua are classic examples of the intricate ecological relationships that can be formed on isolated island chains, but sadly they also show how vulnerable these species and their relationships are. As we humans have colonised these remote islands, we have altered the habitats in which both the trees and the birds live. We have also introduced lots of different species, both plant and animal, and these in turn have had an impact on the native species that had lived there in harmony for millennia. Of the three birds and the tree mentioned above, the crested honeycreeper is the species that has suffered the most, but even the 'ōhi'a lehua tree has suffered due to competition from a whole host of non-native plants and, more recently, a virulent fungal pathogen. We humans do find it all too easy to upset delicate balances.

I don't know how many species of tree depend on birds for their pollination, and I can't imagine that anyone else does, either. There are unquestionably many cases of ornithophily that still await our discovery, especially in the remote tropical locations where birds such as the hummingbirds, sunbirds and Hawaiian honeycreepers dwell, locations where it can be hard to undertake the careful observations needed to ascertain what's happening in the high tree canopies. But not all cases of ornithophily are to be found in the tropics and on remote island chains. One particular example could be happening in your back garden – it's certainly happening in mine.

Because our 'garden' birds are so familiar to us, we tend not to appreciate their beauty in the way we appreciate the beauty of an exotic hummingbird we have never seen before. Many of our common birds are in fact real stunners with fantastically bright colours, but because we see them every day they have become everyday and they have lost their wow factor. Familiarity might not always breed contempt, but it can lead to us taking for granted the real beauty of our commoner birds. This shouldn't be the case. It would be wonderful if we could always look at our common birds as if we were seeing them for the first time.

Blue tit

Imagine if you had lived your entire life in South America and then came to a British garden for the first time and saw a blue tit hanging in a gravity-defying manner off of a twig tip as it searched for food. You would be blown away by its beauty, its grace and its colour palette. Blue tits are true stunners. They are also practitioners of ornithophily; they are pollinators of trees.

The blue tit is such a familiar bird to us that it is easy to forget just how exotic-looking it really is. Let's just remind ourselves. This is a bird with a captivating combination of black and white on its face, topped off with a smart blue cap (brighter in males than in females); its undersides are dressed in yellow, offset with a dark, yet subtle, central strip, and then it has more blue shades on its wings and back. It is truly beautiful.

When we think of a blue tit, we tend to think of a bird that will acrobatically hang off our peanut feeders in the garden, or can be seen hunting the newly emerged leaves on oak trees for those aforementioned small green caterpillars to feed its young with. The birds are mainly insectivorous, resorting to seeds when caterpillars are scarce. We associate these lovely, familiar little birds with feeding on a variety of food sources (including cream) but we don't associate them with feeding on nectar; indeed, we generally don't associate this behaviour with any European species at all.

But blue tits *do* feed on nectar, and they get it from two of the commonest trees in the British Isles: the goat willow and the grey willow. They are closely related and look very

Willow flowers

similar, often causing confusion when it comes to their identification, which is probably the reason they are often just referred to as sallows. The easiest way to tell them apart is to look at their leaves; those of the goat willow are broader, less than twice as long as they are broad, whilst those of the grey willow are slenderer, two to three times as long as they are broad – so identifying the trees is a bit more difficult in winter.

Both of these willow species produce abundant flowers in the early spring, before they come into leaf. It is a showy display for a native British tree – so showy that we have not only noticed it but named it. When they are flowering we refer to them as pussy willows, referring to the soft and furry appearance of the flowers. (That label makes no distinction between the two species, nor does it make any distinction between the two types of flower on show.) Both the goat willow and the grey willow are dioecious.[50] So each of the individual goat and grey willow trees that we see around us is either male or female.

---

50 Meaning that an individual tree produces either male flowers or female flowers, but not both.

Yew tree

This sounds like normality to us mammals, but in the British tree world it isn't. Most of our native tree species are monoecious.[51] Trees like our two native species of oak, our two native species of birch, and the hazel – trees that should be familiar to us all – are monoecious, producing small unobtrusive flowers of both sexes.

The willows aren't the only dioecious trees in Britain, though. Probably the best-known example of this type of tree is the common holly; in the spring these prickly-leaved trees produce either small white male flowers or very similar-looking small female flowers, but never both. It is only the female flowers that go on to produce the holly berries so sought after for Christmas wreaths and garlands. If you have a holly in your garden and you have always wondered why it never produces berries, it is most likely because it's a male tree rather than a female.

---

51 Both male and female flowers are present on the same individual tree.

It is easy to label dioecious trees male or female, but it is not always as clear-cut as that. The common yew, that dark doyen of churchyards, seriously muddies the waters when we start trying to label our trees according to sex. They can be dioecious, producing only male flowers or only female – but they can also be monoecious, an individual tree producing both male and female flowers. Furthermore, a dioecious yew tree that has been only producing male flowers for years, decades and even sometimes centuries, can suddenly stop producing male flowers and start producing female ones instead! Yews, brilliantly anarchic, are yet another example of how nature doesn't always fit in with humanity's neat orderly view of life.

But back to the willows, which remain firmly dioecious. For the female sallows to produce fertile seed, they need to receive the pollen from a male tree. The mechanism for this had been largely overlooked for decades, if not centuries. The flowers are well known as important food sources for early emerging flying insects, particularly queen bumblebees who are waking up from their winter-induced sleep at the time when both species of willow are coming into flower. With their energy resources seriously depleted after hibernation, the queen bees are in rapid need of an energy-fuelling drink and the pussy flowers of the willows are a well-used source of nourishment for these brilliant little insects, which feed voraciously on their sugary nectar. It had always been assumed that in feeding from these flowers the bumblebees were also acting as the main pollinators, although I know of nobody who had actually taken the time to actually study this in any detail. Then, in the late 1970s, the bumblebee pollination hypothesis began to be questioned: were these species of willow (like many trees, including our oaks, birches and the hazel) actually wind-pollinated, a process called anemophily, rather than insect-pollinated?

This prompted further research, and in a 1984 study in an area of allotments and scrub in West Glamorgan, Wales, the biologist Quentin Kay made a discovery that blew the wind pollination debate wide open. Published in the journal *Bird Study* produced by the British Trust for Ornithology (BTO), Kay set the scene:

> The flowers of *Salix* spp. are usually said to be insect-pollinated … but, although bees are common visitors to the catkins and visits by a wide variety of insects have been recorded…, little is known about the pollination biology of *Salix* spp. There is no conclusive evidence that intersex visits resulting in effective pollination are made by the insects. All *Salix* spp. are dioecious and pollen must be transferred from male to female plants for seed-set to take place. It has recently been suggested that *Salix* spp. may in fact be largely wind-pollinated.

As both goat willow and grey willow were abundant in the study area, Quentin Kay and his team began to research exactly how these trees were pollinated. Straightaway it was noted that blue tits made 'substantial' visits to the flowers of both tree species, and that they did so in a much more rapid way than the queen bumblebees that were also seen feeding on the sallow flowers. It was soon realised that the birds were actually visiting far greater numbers of the flowers over the study area than the bees were. Now, it had long been known that blue tits frequented the flowers of both goat and grey willow, but the reasons behind these visits had never been fully resolved, some studies suggesting that they were feeding on the flowers themselves and others suggesting that they were feeding on the insects that had been attracted to the flowers. So, whilst it was no surprise to see blue tits visiting the flowers of the trees, what Quentin Kay and his team were actually witnessing, in his own words, 'was completely unexpected'.

As part of the study into how the trees were pollinated. Quentin Kay had already shown that both the male and the female flowers of both tree species produced substantial amounts of nectar, and he described how, unlike most flowers that hide their sugary reward away, this nectar would form large droplets that were visible even to human eyes. Of course, if these sweet sugary nectar drops were visible to our eyes, they would also be readily visible to the eyes of the blue tit, as well as being easily accessible to their small beaks.

The flowers of both species of willow grow in aggregations known as catkins, comprising over 100 individual inflorescences. After witnessing blue tits visiting the catkins, Kay examined the flowers carefully, finding abundant evidence that the birds were indeed feeding on the nectar of the flowers, as opposed to feeding on the flowers themselves or on any insects that might happen to be on them.

Through his observations, he also noted that blue tits did indeed visit both the male and female flower-bearing trees and that at times they even travelled up to 80 metres between them. Detailed watching of the birds also revealed that they were liberally dusted with the pollen from the male flowers, indicating that pollen transfer was indeed happening as a result of the blue tit's feeding on the tree's nectar. Not only did this study reveal proof that ornithophily was happening, but also it showed that the birds were much more efficient at pollinating the flowers than the bumblebees were; an individual blue tit when foraging would individually visit over three and a half times more catkins in a timed minute than a bumblebee would and, because the birds would regularly fly many metres between trees during their foraging, the likelihood of pollen transfer from male flower to female flower was greatly increased. A bumblebee, however, might spend all its time feeding on flowers on one tree, these would all be flowers of the same sex due to the dioecious nature of the willows, and therefore pollination would not occur.

It is now widely accepted, but very rarely talked about, that the goat willow and the grey willow, two of our most common native trees, are indeed pollinated by the blue tit in much the same way as many tropical trees are pollinated by hummingbirds, sunbirds and Hawaiian honeycreepers. So ornithophily isn't just a far-off tropical phenomenon – it can happen on our doorsteps. That isn't to say that the goat willow and the grey willow rely solely on blue tits for their pollination. Insects, including the aforementioned bumblebees, also play a role in doing so; these are trees that don't put all their eggs in one basket.

But perhaps these trees help the blue tit put eggs in their own nest. As part of the study, Kay quoted other studies that had calculated the daily calorific requirements of the blue tit.

On average, these studies had shown that each of these small birds needs 10.8 kcal (10,800 calories) per day to carry out its normal behaviour. He and his team then calculated the calorific content of the nectar produced by the two species of willow and worked out that a blue tit could obtain its total daily calorific requirement in just three hours and twenty minutes of feeding on the nectar of the trees.

Quentin Kay didn't take this any further in his study, but as I read the paper my brain started wandering off along trails of wonder. The relationship between goat and grey willow and the blue tit obviously benefits both partners – the trees get pollinated and the birds get fed – but is there more to it than that? Are the blue tits getting other benefits from their springtime sugar-rich suppings?

Obviously no bird is able to spend over three hours continuously feeding without doing anything else, but foraging in the early spring, when food resources may be harder to find, does take up the vast majority of the time that these little birds spend active. Goat and grey willows flower in March and into early April. The spring equinox occurs on 20 March, meaning that at that point we are experiencing 12 hours of daylight in each 24-hour period. That's plenty of time for a blue tit to carry out three hours and twenty minutes of nectar feeding. Early spring is often thought of as being a particularly difficult time for small insectivorous birds; after all, there is a real lack of invertebrate food available, which is why many of our insect-eating migrants arrive after the end of March. But if a bird was able to supplement its insect-based diet with an abundance of sugary nectar during March, then that potentially difficult time could instead become a time of plenty.

The nectar of the willows would not just allow the blue tits to easily consume their minimum daily calorie requirement, but it could also enable them to overconsume calories, building their bodies up for something else – something that takes a lot of calorific reserves to successfully achieve. Breeding. Blue tits lay their clutches in April, immediately after the nectar-rich feeding potential of the goat and grey willow flowers has passed. Could that be linked? I am inclined to think so. The female blue tit, weighing no more than 11 grams – one gram less than a £2 coin – lays on average between eight and ten eggs. Each of those eggs in turn weighs, on average, 1.1 grams. The female blue tit is therefore effectively laying her own body weight.

To do so just after a time when insects are few and far between must surely make huge demands on this small bird's physiology. So surely the easy energy obtained from the nectar of goat and grey willows must play a part in the breeding cycle of the blue tit. How can it not? I have no proof. I'm no researcher, and it's just speculation on my part, the wandering wondering of my grey matter. But the goat and grey willows have already evolved a relationship with the blue tit in which one benefits the other, a relationship that went unnoticed by us until only recently. So there is no reason that I can see why this relationship might not be a bit more in depth than we first thought. It would be interesting to see whether blue tits that have had access to goat and grey willow flowers lay bigger clutches than those that don't, or whether the hatching rate for the broods laid by birds that have been feeding on nectar is higher compared to those that haven't.

Blue tits are widely known to time their breeding with the emergence of the caterpillars of the winter moth and the green tortrix moth. These caterpillars hatch out to coincide with the young oak leaves bursting out from the protection of the buds in which they have developed. There is certainly plenty of evidence that shows that a higher percentage of blue tit chicks fledge when there is an abundance of these small caterpillars for the adults to feed to them. The availability of caterpillars influences the numbers of blue tit chicks that fledge. But as far as I can find out, there has been no research carried out on what influences the potential size of the clutch in the first place. Is it possible that the breeding ecology of the blue tit involves the flowers of the willows just as much as it involves the leaf-eating caterpillars of the oaks?

The year 2021 was a not a good one for the blue tit; April was exceptionally dry and particularly cold, especially at night; the leaves of the oaks were much later in their emergence, and as a result the hatching of the caterpillars was also delayed. But the blue tits didn't, or couldn't, delay their breeding; their clutches were laid at the normal time. To make it worse for the birds, when the leaves finally did emerge, May was one of the wettest ever, the heavy and almost continuous rain washing the caterpillars from the leaves and making foraging for food by the adult birds nigh on impossible. From all across the country there came reports of blue tit nests failing; the eggs had been laid as normal and they had hatched as normal, but the chicks had starved in the nest before they could fledge, despite the frantic and desperate efforts of the adults. In our own nest box in the garden we found the distressing sight of eight shrivelled and dead blue tit chicks, unfortunate victims of the vagaries of the weather.

But why hadn't the blue tits been able to delay their laying? Was it because the flowers of the goat and grey willows had been on time, producing the nectar in March as normal, providing the food source required for the female blue tits to get into breeding condition – only for the next chain in the link to fail? It is yet more speculation, I admit, but the ecology of individual species and their relationships with others is highly intricate, and there is so much we don't know, even about the species that are so common we take them for granted.

The goat willow is an integral component of the British countryside, and it has been here for a lot longer than many other trees. The pollen records shows that as the last glaciation retreated, but before the land bridge with the continent was inundated and lost, the goat willow was one of the first tree species to colonise the land that is now Britain. As its tiny seeds are wind-borne they can be carried long distances by the currents of the air; it is the archetypal pioneer species, able to rapidly establish itself on open ground. And as the ice sheets melted away and the tundra retreated, plenty of ground became available for species that had been previously frozen out.

But the receding of the ice sheets didn't mean that the air temperature had become warm. It meant that it had become less cold. Studies have estimated that at the time that the goat willow was leading the vanguard of trees heading north to Britain, the air temperatures were lower than they are today by a few degrees. When the goat willow comes into flower in March, the modern-day temperature can often be chilly, but while the ice sheets were retreating, that air temperature would have been considerably colder.

Early emerging queen bumblebees will fly in air temperatures as low as 10°C, but it is not ideal for them, and they struggle to keep their flight muscles warm enough in such low temperatures. To keep those small but powerful muscles working, they need to be able to maintain an internal thorax temperature of 30°C; remarkably, they can do this, but it is very energy-demanding, and their ability to be effective pollinators in these sorts of temperatures must surely be compromised.

But 10°C is the average air temperature of March in the UK today, and as we have seen, back when the goat willow was colonising what would become the UK the average temperature would have been lower than that. It is therefore likely that it was blue tits and not bumblebees that played the key role in the pollination of the goat willow as it raced towards what would become the British Isles, getting here ahead of the main arboreal cohort. Blue tits and the goat willow (and the closely related grey willow) have a relationship that is as old as the hills themselves.

You will have noticed that there has been one common denominator with trees that are pollinated by birds: the colour red. The vast majority of flowers pollinated by hummingbirds, sunbirds and Hawaiian honeycreepers are in the red band of the colour spectrum. But as with every rule there are exceptions, and the flowers of the goat and grey willows are an exception, being yellowy-gold in the male flowers and more silvery in the female ones. However, as mentioned earlier, they make up for the lack of redness by visually displaying the nectar reward in the form of droplets big enough to catch the eye, just as the red petals of a flower may do. But as it is red that's the normal colour used by trees to attract birds, not just for pollination but also for propagation, that is what we will look at next.

Seeing red

The flowers on the trees have been pollinated, the seed is set. There is one thing more that needs to happen before those seeds can fulfil their potential; they need to find somewhere to grow. Trees spread their seed by many means; some use ocean currents, some use the wind. There are others that use mammals and even some that use insects, and of course, a lot of them use birds. In my garden in Devon I have a guelder rose, a small tree that's a member of the viburnum family; it is a relatively common, if often unnoticed, native tree in Britain.

Guelder roses are attractive additions to any garden; they have straight pale stems that fork geometrically, giving good structure. In the spring the clusters of their creamy flowers are an attractive focal point, whilst in autumn the foliage puts on a spectacular show of colour, and as these leaves finally drop the fruits, the berries, come into their own, going a beautiful bright red, vibrant as glacé cherries. Whilst this attractive native is a great arboreal feature to have in a garden, I didn't plant it. Its addition wasn't deliberate. This is a tree

Guelder rose

that has turned up in my garden without human help.

I am not aware of any other guelder rose growing nearby. There certainly aren't any within sight of the garden – but there must be at least one that is relatively close, and I am confident that it will be within about 20 minutes of thrush-foraging time from my garden. Looking at where this guelder rose is growing, I am confident, in the best possible Sherlock Holmes manner, that I can deduce that a bird is responsible for depositing the seed that led to the tree. It is growing between the common hazel and the goat willow, both of which offer perfect bird perches immediately over the spot where the guelder rose germinated. I can just picture the bird, sitting on one of these perches and letting its digestive system expel the seed.

But even without channelling my inner Sherlock, I know that it's a bird that propagated this tree, because the berries of the guelder rose are red.

Red is the colour that trees (and plants in general) employ if they want to engage the services of birds. From the red flowers of trees on the Hawaiian islands to the red berries in my own back garden, trees use red to attract birds, either for pollination or for propagation. There are exceptions – there are always exceptions – but if you find a tree with red berries, it's a safe bet that it relies to at least some degree on birds to distribute the seed within.

Red is a signal for birds, but for me the colour is not an easy one to see. I have Daltonism; I am colour-blind.[52] This means that for me at least, items or animals that are camouflaged are easier to see than for other people. But obvious (to normal eyes) items, like an orange on a lawn, can be virtually impossible for me to pick out. I have difficulties with colours right across the spectrum, but for me the red spectrum is particularly problematic. I have even mistaken someone bleeding badly from their hand for someone who'd had a goat with diarrhoea defecate on them – a long story, but suffice to say I'd make a very bad forensic scientist.

---

52 I am not blind to colour itself. It's just that even though we all, even those of us who aren't colour-blind, see colours differently to one another, I see some colours very differently from what the majority of other people see.

Some people that aren't colour-blind find it very difficult to understand what I see – it baffles and confuses them. Humans tend, too, to think that other species, even completely unrelated ones like the avian dinosaurs, see the world as we see it. Which they don't. If you can't understand how a fellow human who is colour-blind sees the world, then you are highly unlikely to understand how completely unrelated animals, ones that see colours beyond our own visible range, see it.

Colours are basically wavelengths of the electromagnetic spectrum that fall within the range of human sight, and are called visible light. They form just a small part of the whole spectrum rather than the whole of it. The colours we see fall in between the wavelengths of 400 and 700 nanometres.[53] These colours are the ones we learn at school via the Richard Of York Gave Battle In Vain mnemonic – which, incidentally, is the only way that I know the order of colours in a rainbow – red, orange, yellow, green, blue, indigo and violet. To see these colours, humans have three retinal cone photoreceptors, giving us trichromatic vision.

But birds have tetrachromatic vision – four retinal cone photoreceptors. This addition to their colour vision perception enables them to see in the range 300–700 nm,[54] which includes ultra-violet, something we can't perceive. Not only does that extra photoreceptor enable birds to see more colours than we can, but it also enables them to see the colours that fall within our 400–700 nm range in a far greater depth of richness than we can ever perceive. At least, that's what scientists in that field think. The fact is, it's impossible for us humans to know exactly what birds see, or how their brains interpret the signals they receive from their eyes. We still don't even fully comprehend the structure of birds' eyes; they have, for example, something within them that we have named a double cone, yet we don't really understand what its function is.

What we do know, though, is that birds see the world differently from us; they can see outwith our own visible spectrum, they can see things we can't, and they also see the things that we can see differently from the way we see them. Trying to conceive how a bird sees the world is impossible for us; we can use technology to help, to give us an idea, but in reality we just don't know the exact details. We might not know how birds see the colour red, but we know that they do see it, and we know that it plays a key role in the relationship between them and trees.

The perfect package

When we think of birds distributing the seeds of trees we invariably think of the berry, the perfect package for a seed distributed by birds. But before we look more closely at that, allow me to define what I mean by the word 'berry'. You might think it would be easy.

---

53 A nanometre is one billionth of a metre, which is rather short.

54 Bioscience article 50/10/854/233996

But no. To begin with, not all berries are berries, because unlike trees, there are hard and fast biological rules for defining what makes a berry a berry. Botanically speaking, a berry is a fruit that has a fleshy pulp and seeds produced from the ovary of a single flower. That sounds simple enough, but it has implications relating to what we refer to, biologically speaking, as berries. For example, if we follow that definition, then bananas, avocados,[55] aubergines and cucumbers are all berries, even though the vast majority of us don't tend to think of them as being so. Conversely, blackberries, strawberries, sloes (from the blackthorn) and yew berries are not berries, even though we call them that. Technically speaking, the blackberry is actually an etaerio or aggregate fruit; the strawberry is an example of an achene or accessory fruit; the sloe is a drupe; and the yew berry is a cone.

Our human obsession with order and neatness, and the subsequent rules and categories we create for the natural world, means that defining what we mean by a berry can create confusion, so to keep things simple I am going to use the term 'berry' in its common usage: a fleshy fruit with a seed or seeds in it.

The berry, then, is a great example of a mutualistic symbiotic relationship. It is a relationship that evolved millions of years ago, the earliest fossils demonstrating the presence of berries dating to around 66 million years ago.[56] I don't know how the relationship evolved. It could have been that fruit-eating species came first, driving the trees and the plants that existed at that time to evolve ever more tempting fruits. But perhaps the reverse is true; the trees and the plants evolved the fruits as a package in which to protect their seed as they ripened and that fruit-eaters evolved to then exploit this food source. Or it could have been a combination of the two, fruit and fruit eaters coevolving.

Whatever the origins of the relationship, it has come a long way since, and is now a very common form of seed dispersal for many trees, including several British natives such as the rowan, the whitebeam, the hawthorn and the blackthorn. Scientifically speaking, the relationship is an example of endozoochory. It's a very simple relationship; the tree provides a fleshy parcel full of calories and vitamins for the bird to consume, and the bird acts as a courier (albeit one that is a bit random in its delivery) distributing the tree's seed away from the immediate vicinity of the parent.

It is simple, it is effective and it is also key to the ecology of many species of trees and birds across the globe. Many tree seeds need a period of dormancy before they generate, and in the UK our winter provides that,[57] with the seed germinating in the spring as the days lengthen and the temperature increases. Producing seed requires an energetic investment on

---

55 The avocado that we eat is actually the fruit of a tree that originated in Mexico, which can grow to a height of 20 metres or more.

56 That meteorite date again!

57 Although some take longer; the seeds of the bird cherry, another British native, can lie dormant for up to five years before germinating.

the part of the tree, first producing the flowers that need to be pollinated and then producing the fruit and seed. This of course takes time, which means that the fruit isn't ready to be taken until the autumn and winter months. This fits in with the dormancy requirements of the seed, and it also fits very nicely with the feeding requirements of the birds.

Birds such as the blackbird and the song thrush eat a lot of worms and snails during the spring and the summer, but as autumn arrives this food supply gradually becomes harder to find; the lower temperatures push worms deeper underground, and snails head off to a hibernaculum to see out the winter months sealed in their shells. There is then a lack of invertebrate food for these (and many other) birds, so they need to switch diets – and they do so, turning their attention to the abundance of berries that are just coming to fruition on our trees. For the thrushes (which include the blackbird), the availability of berries over the winter months is absolutely vital to their prospects of surviving to the following spring.

In Britain, our trees provide vast quantities of berries for the birds every autumn and winter; this abundance is reflected in the numbers of thrushes that, joining our resident birds, migrate here from further north and east. Fieldfare and redwing arrive in their millions,[58] attracted by the fruit borne by our trees, in particular the hawthorn, blackthorn, holly, yew and rowan. Our berries are a food source worth flying thousands of miles for.

The flesh of the fruit is an inducement, and once the payment has been swallowed, the birds perform their side of the bargain; the seeds may be cleaned of their nutritious flesh in the bird's gizzard before being coughed up and ejected, or otherwise they pass through the digestive system and, cleaned, are ejected in the bird's faecal matter. Both processes take time, which means that the bird has usually moved some distance from the tree that bore the fruit, fulfilling the distribution requirement. Of course, berry-eating birds don't carefully deposit the seeds from the fruit in propitious places – it's a random scattering of seed – but as far as the tree is concerned it's a numbers game. A mature hawthorn can have thousands of berries on offer, and the odds are that some of the seed will land – often embedded within its own fertiliser package courtesy of the bird's digestive tract – in a spot where it will be able to germinate successfully.

Berries such as those on the hawthorn take their time to ripen. The seed within them needs to develop until it becomes viable, and whilst this is happening the fruit of the berry is green, like the myriad leaves that cover the tree. It is only when the seed inside is ready that the flesh of the berry turns the familiar red. It is a signal to the birds and one that they recognise, but the birds don't interpret the signal as meaning that the seed within the berry is ready for distribution – they interpret it as meaning that the flesh around the seed is now tasty and packed full of nutrition. If birds fed on the berries before the seed was ready, then the tree wouldn't have viable seed distributed by the bird, so the flesh of the berry only ripens, changing colour, once the seed is ready. Birds avoid eating green berries for the same reason

---

58 The RSPB estimates the average number of redwings in the UK in winter at 8.6 million; fieldfare are fewer, coming in at around 680,000 birds.

we don't eat unripe fruits; they don't taste good.[59]

Trees such as the hawthorn, the yew, the holly and the rowan have berries that ripen with the tree in leaf; the red that is used by these species to signify that their fruit is ripe (and therefore that the seed is ready) is one that stands out against the green of the leaves, particularly so for birds, who seem to quickly notice the colour change – flocks of thrushes will rapidly descend on areas of trees that have turned their fruits red. Although we may be only able to speculate how birds see the world, the red fruit against the green of the leaves is evidently extremely eye-catching to them.

There is even evidence to suggest that the type of red that the bird can see has an influence on its decision to feed on particular trees. A study of hawthorn berries has shown that not all haws, as they are known, are equal; the nutritional elements of these fruits can vary from tree to tree, perhaps even from berry to berry. Some are high in sugars, some high in fat (lipids). Haws high in sugar provide a quick burst of energy, something that might be useful to birds after a long cold night, while those that are high in lipids will provide a slower, more sustained, burn of energy, helping the birds get through the long cold night in the first place.

---

59 It might be just me, but I find it interesting that in this relationship green signifies stop and red go.

Hawthorn berries

Of the Trees and the Birds

In winter 2020, during a rare cold snap before Christmas, I went out for an early morning walk, enjoying the high-pressure crispness of the air and the beautiful birding light that it brings. I didn't go far – just a quick walk along the lanes that radiate from the village. Rooks populated the fields, busy feeding and chattering to one another in their distinctive voices as yet more of them flew in; clusters of starlings whizzed by in tight formation; and everywhere the chuckling call of fieldfare hung in the air. There are plenty of hawthorns around the village, and that year they were bedecked in berries, a bumper crop that attracted a bumper number of fieldfares, redwings and blackbirds. On that cold morning, it didn't take me long to find some of these thrushes; large numbers of all three species had descended into the straggly mass of hawthorns that grow alongside the river on the edge of the village, the trees were literally covered in the birds, all of them busy feeding and occasionally bickering, gleaning the goodness of the fruit and unwittingly stocking up on seed to disperse.

Fieldfare

When I returned later in the afternoon, the sky had remained clear, the temperature had stayed low and a cold wind was mischievously nipping away at my fingers as I carried my camera in the hope of getting some nice shots of the birds as they fed in the lowering sunlight. The trees still retained berries, although greatly depleted – but they hadn't retained the birds. Not one thrush to be seen. Bemoaning my usual photographic luck, I headed back to the village, this time by another lane. Along the way I stopped off in a gateway, and as I looked out over the pastoral landscape I spotted a large group of thrushes feeding on more hawthorns in the distance. Too far for a photo – typical! – but good to see nonetheless.

Thinking back to that day now, I find myself wondering about why the birds were where they were. There are of course dozens of potential reasons for the birds to use one area in the morning and a different area in the afternoon, but one of those reasons could well have been the quality of the red that the birds perceived as they flew over the landscape. Were the haws in the clump by the river attractive to the thrushes in the morning because their shade showed that they had a high sugar content and were therefore able to give the birds a much-needed sugary boost after a long dark cold night? Were the haws on the trees in the afternoon displaying another shade, advertising a high content of more sustaining nourishment in the form of lipids, just the right sort of food to consume before the onset of another long dark cold night? I don't know – after all, I find it difficult enough to spot the red of haws amongst the green of the tree's remaining leaves, so there's no way I'm going to spot subtleties of shades – but it is an intriguing thought, and perhaps what I witnessed on that cold day could have been an example of how birds see things differently.

However the birds see and interpret the red of berries, there is no doubt that the colour red draws birds in from distance. A good example of this are the rowan trees planted in many supermarket car parks. The trees are planted for our benefit; they are amenity trees, planted to prettify what is otherwise a pretty bleak landscape of tarmac, white lines and trolley stations, and they are often some distance away from good bird habitat. But as soon as their berries ripen, they become a mecca for birds.

We humans have long known that birds are attracted to red berries and we have exploited it for our own gain. The second part of the rowan's scientific name is *aucuparia*, which derives from the Latin for 'bird', *avis*, and 'to catch', *capere*: 'bird catcher'. The tree is well named.[60]

The berries of the rowan are packed full of nourishment, particularly high in Vitamin C,[61] and the thrushes' predilection for the fruits was all too easily exploited by humans seeking food of their own. Simple wooden traps were baited with the berries, and the birds were caught alive. They were once a popular bird for the pot. Thankfully no longer, at least in this country – but unfortunately they are still regularly killed in many other countries for food, a practice that is still legal if not ethical.

---

60 Scientifically, at least; its alternative English name, mountain ash, is an example of an inappropriate name, for the rowan is unrelated to the ashes (which are in fact closely related to olives).

61 We've long known this too, a concoction made from them was given to sailors in the past to help prevent scurvy.

Thrushes aren't the only group of birds drawn to the berries of the rowan; several members of the crow family will also feed on them, taking advantage of their seasonal abundance. They too propagate the tree, depositing the seed from which new rowans will germinate. We don't tend to think of corvids as being distributors of seed (apart from the jay, which we will look at later) but they too can play an important role in the distribution of tree seed. In some places in Scotland there is a phrase, 'craa-sown', describing the otherwise unlikely appearance of young rowans growing in open ground. It means 'sown by crows', and is probably very often accurate in its description.

Yew will be punished

The yew is probably my favourite species of tree. They are fantastic arboreal beings, anarchic in their nature, dark and brooding however they grow, each one taking on its own form. Some are compact, others open-crowned with sprawling branches; some are single-stemmed, others multi-stemmed; some reach for the skies, others stay squat in the landscape; they are scruffy, they are tidy. This unruliness of form, this disregard for the rules, is also, as we have already seen, repeated in their biology. They disregard the meaning of biological terms like monoecious and dioecious, individual trees making individual reproductive choices. Even their growth stubbornly refuses to conform to how we expect a tree to grow.

There is no doubt that yew trees are capable of obtaining great age, but exactly how old is a subject that has led to much debate and lots of guesses, often very wild ones. Most species of trees grow at a predictable rate, which means that when we have measured its girth and factored in where it is growing, we can calculate a ballpark figure of its age. But not the yew; it has its very own unique way of growing. Of course it does.

Every yew tree is an idiosyncratic individual, and their growth rates can fluctuate wildly. Generally speaking they are slow growers, which is why we automatically assign great ages to large ones, but sometimes a yew can start growing prodigiously and continue to do so for many years, growing at a rate that belies the generally slow growth. But, then, without warning, it will suddenly change tack and revert to the more usual slow growth of the species. Sometimes a yew tree will seemingly stop altogether, hardly growing at all for decades. These periods of senescence can make you think that the tree is in terminal decline, on its way out – but then, suddenly, unpredictably, it will find a new lease of life, growing once more, sending out new shoots and putting on girth. Nothing is consistent about the growth of yews, and that renders it impossible to extrapolate their ages from measurements, because we have no way of knowing how fast or how slowly the tree has grown in the past. They are true arboreal iconoclasts. They follow no rules.

There are some great specimens of yew in Britain and it is generally accepted that there are some that are around, or even over, 2,000 years old – but we have no way of ascertaining this. You will see much written about the ages of various yews in this country – numbers that are often stated as hard facts – but the reality is that those figures are just conjecture. I have already mentioned how trees hollow out as they get older. The yew does actually follow this general rule, but in doing so it thwarts any chance of getting an accurate age from it. The only certain way to age a tree is to count its growth rings,[62] if its hollow centre means that there are no rings to count, you can't age a tree.

But does their age actually matter? Of course it doesn't! We don't need to know the exact age of a tree to appreciate its beauty and its venerable status. These arboreal beasts don't need arbitrary labels – they just need our appreciation.

Yews are a conifer, the group of trees that significantly pre-date the broadleaves. Yews are one of only three conifers that are native to the British Isles, although many more have subsequently been introduced. The name 'conifer' literally means 'cone bearing', referring to the seeds of the tree being borne in protective cones whilst they develop. In this the yew *does* follow the rules, it does bear cones – but being the rebel that it is, the yew does so with a twist. Those red berries that the female, male and female (or once-male-now-female) trees produce are actually highly modified cone structures known as arils, with the sticky sweet red flesh protecting the seed within in much the same way that the woody exterior of a typical pine cone does.

As well as being well known for potentially being of great age, the yew is also famous for being poisonous. The tree's bark, the tree's leaves (needles), the timber itself, the pollen, the seed and even the sawdust produced when cutting the wood, are all poisonous; virtually every single part of these brilliant trees are toxic to us, potentially deadly. If we were to consume the tree's leaves or eat the seeds we would become seriously ill and quite likely die. But there is one part of the tree that isn't poisonous; the bright red aril that surrounds the seed. Yew berries are not poisonous to us. But as the small seed within it is – and potentially lethally so – we humans learnt long ago not to be tempted by the sweet lure of the fruit; it's a dangerous temptress.

But then, that sweet red flesh was never meant to be consumed by us, or any other mammal. It's the inducement and payment for seed distribution by birds, and by birds alone. If I put my anthropomorphic head on for a moment, I could look on the yew as a tree that doesn't follow rules itself, but expects others to follow the rules it sets for its seed distribution. The seeds are meant for birds; if a mammal tries to get in on the act it is killed. So it won't do it again. After all, nature is red in tooth and claw, as well as in berries.[63]

The seed of the yew passes undamaged through the avian gut, but the mammalian gut is

---

62 You don't need to fell a tree to count its rings; specially designed increment borers are used to extract a ring core, which can then be counted.

63 The yew is not the only native British tree to load its seeds with toxin to deter the wrong kind of seed-disperser. The beautiful spindle is a common tree that largely passes under the radar. For most of the year it is an unseen component of our countryside, but in the autumn it is adorned with eye-catching pink Chinese lantern-like fruit cases complete with bright orange seeds. They look spectacular. As we will see later, the spindle requires its seed to pass through a bird's gut, not a mammalian one. To us mammals, spindle poisoning can be just as fatal as yew poisoning.

too robust for it, breaking down the seed casing and destroying the embryonic tree within and releasing its lethal toxins. There is no advantage for the yew if a mammal eats its fruit and seed, and it would appear that the tree most certainly doesn't convey any advantage on any mammal that tries it.

The relationship between the yew and the birds is highly evolved to ensure the maximum benefit for both parties. Yews depend on birds to distribute their seeds, and many species of birds depend on yews to provide them with food throughout the difficult winter months. Unlike the hawthorn and the rowan, though, the yew doesn't produce all of its berries in one glut; it staggers the production of them over a period of about three months from around mid-November, providing thrushes, waxwings, starlings, corvids and the like with a steady supply of ripening berries throughout the lean winter period.

Yews are of course evergreen, like the holly, and the red of both of their berries are easily detected by the birds against the constant green background of the foliage. But some trees that have evolved relationships with birds to distribute their seeds don't ripen their fruits until after the leaves have either fallen or gone dormant. When this happens, red is not always the key colour.

Unseen signals

The blackthorn is a very common tree across Britain, Europe and western Asia. It is a member of the *Prunus* genus, the cherries – but unlike the sweet and juicy fruits of the cultivated cherries we enjoy, the fruits of the blackthorn are extremely sour to our taste buds. They are not red when ripe, either; they are purple-black.

Sloe-laden blackthorn amongst hazel leaves

Berries that ripen after the leaves have fallen, or after the leaves have faded and yellowed, or withered and gone brown, tend to be black rather than red. It is thought that in these conditions this darker colouration of the fruit is more noticeable to birds than red. Although not a tree, ivy is a good example of this; its berries are packed full of calories – so full in fact that if we ate such calorie-loaded food (please don't, they are poisonous) we would soon grow obese. Ivy berries ripen in the winter after the plant's foliage has gone dormant, and as they do so they too turn purple-black. Birds love them, and they provide an important food source for many species, which in turn distribute the seeds freely.

As previously mentioned, we only have three species of conifer native to Britain. Of these, the yew has red berries; the Scots pine has typical brown cones so beloved of children's cone fights; and the third, the juniper, has purple-blue berries when ripe. The common juniper, to give it its full name (there are around 50 species of juniper) is the most naturally widespread of all extant tree species, with a global distribution spanning the entire northern hemisphere. It is very variable in form, sometimes forming upright trees of around 10 metres in height, sometimes forming a prostrate carpet of spiky foliage. Like the yew, its berries are actually highly modified cones, but unlike the yew its seeds are not poisonous to us, although we would find them extremely astringent.[64] The juniper is evergreen, but it too has the dark purple-black colouration for its fruits; this is a colour that evidently stands out against the tree's grey green spiky foliage better than red would, at least in the eyes of the birds that feed on the berries. Juniper berries take a long time to mature; they start off green, but they don't fully ripen for around 18 months, although they will often be purple-black to our eyes long before they are taken by birds.

In the winter it is not unusual to see sloes on blackthorn trees persisting even after the red hawthorn berries have been completely stripped by foraging birds. Like the juniper, sloes appear to us to be the purple-black colour that signifies ripeness, but the birds still wait … I often see blackthorn laden with sloes well into the winter months, the birds seemingly avoiding them, but then they suddenly turn their attention to them, stripping the trees of their fruits. To my eyes nothing has changed in the appearance of the small fruits, yet the birds start to feed on them; either they are being capricious in nature or they are seeing a signal that I am missing.

Nature isn't capricious. I don't see the signal that the trees send the birds to tell them that the berries are ready, because unlike the birds I can't see ultraviolet. Have a close look at sloes on a blackthorn near you, and you will see that some of them have an almost powdery bloom on their surface; the same happens to juniper berries. It is this bloom that signifies that the seed within has fully developed and that the flesh of the fruit is ripe for the plucking. We have to look hard to see the bloom, and so would the birds if it wasn't for the fact that it reflects ultraviolet light, creating a highly visible sign to those that can see in this part of the spectrum. When birds fly over areas of juniper or blackthorn laden with ripe fruit they

---

64 As are the sloes, yet both combine to give us a fine winter's tipple: sloe gin.

cannot fail to notice the tree's signal. How it actually appears to the bird is pure speculation on our part, but it must stand out like a sore thumb, the UV glow of the ripe berries an arboreal equivalent of the yellow jacket of a construction site.

This is why the birds seem to be choosy about when they feed on such berries; they are waiting to see the UV glow that tells them they are ready. They are not being choosy at all, it's just that we can't see the signal. Our thinking that these darker berries stand out better to birds in the winter compared to the red berries of other species that contrast with green foliage was only partly right; it's not the purple-black that we see that stands out – it's the ultra-violet the berries reflect – which we cannot see – that does.

Damaged in transit

As shown when discussing the yew and its propagation, the berry-eating bird's digestive system is relatively simple when compared to that of us mammals. Part of this simplicity is the speed in which food passes through the bird's gut. The seed is not in transit for very long. If a blackbird eats a yew berry the seed will pass through the bird in approximately 30 minutes; but if you were to eat a yew berry (please don't) it could take between 12 and 72 hours to pass through your digestive system.[65] But in fact it wouldn't pass through, because in that time the mammalian digestive processes would have gone to work and the acid in your stomach would have broken down the seed's hard case – bad news for both the yew and you.

But 30 minutes is just enough time for the bird's digestive system to strip off and process the flesh of the berry, whilst the seed continues through, relatively unscathed by its journey. This is typical of most examples of bird/tree propagation. The seed passes intact through the avian gut and comes out the other end, to land potentially in a site where it will then be able to germinate. Although the seed may pass intact through the bird's gut, that doesn't mean that it does so undamaged. But getting damaged in transit is not necessarily a bad thing for a seed – it can actually be important for the seed to get damaged, as it can expedite the process of germination. Seeds that pass through the gut of birds as part of the propagation process are often referred to by horticulturalists as being deeply dormant. If you are a tree grower harvesting seed direct from the tree, this means that you can have a very long wait for the seeds to germinate.

Take holly as an example: the female trees produce their berries after about 20 years; each berry has four small seeds within it, and when these are fully developed, the flesh of the berry ripens to red. On the edge of our garden we have a female holly which produces a steady quantity of berries most years, and as they redden they become a source of friction between our local blackbirds, who spend a considerable amount of time chasing each other around the tree as they try and claim, then defend, rights to the tree's bounty.

Nearby I have a raised vegetable bed in which I grow a variety of foodstuffs for ourselves.

---

65 On average, food takes around 36 hours to pass through a typical human digestive tract.

In the late autumn, as the holly berries ripen nicely, I finish my harvest and give the soil a light rake-over, fishing out any weeds before adding our home-made compost to it, ready for the following spring. We have a particularly tame male blackbird that readily exploits us for food, and he is always in the vicinity of the veg bed when I'm working on it. My autumnal activity often uncovers plenty of worms and other invertebrates; he has learnt this, and as I work over one end of the bed he will stand at the other, always on the alert for the appearance of a wriggly meal. He spends many minutes on the veg bed as I work, and whilst there, he defecates relatively frequently onto the soil. Examination of this soiled soil reveals the presence of seeds.

Each spring as my chard leafs up and my onions grow bigger, I find myself weeding out young holly seedlings that have appeared amongst the veg; with them I find myself pulling up young hawthorn seedlings too – progeny, no doubt, of the two large hawthorns we have on our other garden boundary. The blackbird clearly loves the hawthorn and holly berries just as much as the worms I uncover. It is, if you like, a very practical lesson in just how efficient the tree and bird propagation relationship can be.

Yet if I delve into one of my many silviculture manuals and look up how to grow holly from seed I find something along the lines of the following: 'the seed is deeply dormant and will need to be stored carefully at a temperature of 15°C for ten months followed by storage of another six months at a lower temperature of 4°C'; a total of 16 months of carefully controlled storage that is required to wake up the dormant seed of the holly. Our tame blackbird sorts it out in 30 minutes.

The hawthorn is another tree that has a reputation for having very dormant seeds; even the godfather of silviculture, John Evelyn,[66] wrote that you shouldn't feel despair when your planted haws do not germinate, adding that they can and do spend two years 'imprisoned' under the earth before they finally 'peep' through. But this isn't the case when they get planted by a blackbird; then, they peep through from their supposed earthbound prison the following spring, as soon as the sun's warmth encourages them to do so.

It is a tale repeated for many of the trees that I have already mentioned in this section; if birds feed on the berries of a tree it is likely that that tree's seeds will be described by us humans as 'deeply dormant'. As well as the hawthorn and the holly, trees like elder, guelder rose, yew and blackthorn all have the reputation for having seeds that are deeply dormant, seeds that require lengthy periods of time in careful storage before they will germinate. The beautiful spindle is a tree that I mentioned earlier in a footnote to the yew. I have long wanted one to grow in my garden. I have lost count of how many times I have tried to grow this small native tree from seed that I have collected as I have been out and about. The seeds are very poisonous, so if you try and collect any yourself be very careful – but, to be honest,

---

66 John Evelyn, 1620–1706, was a keen promoter of trees and their silviculture. His book, *Sylva*, published in 1664, is a classic as well as being a plea for people to plant more trees. Facsimile copies are widely available for free on the internet.

you're wasting your time. The seeds are described as being deeply dormant, and they really are; I have never been able to get one to germinate from seed.

From the human point of view, it would appear that these trees must struggle to germinate and grow at all, but as we know – and as a quick walk in the countryside will show – these trees don't struggle. They are common, sometimes very common. You can find them freely germinating and growing throughout the country. I might not be able to get a spindle to germinate, but it is evident that plenty of them do. We humans might struggle to get these tree seeds to germinate, but nature doesn't struggle, because nature uses a mechanism that evolved long ago, long before anything vaguely human descended from the trees; it uses birds and their digestive system. We struggle simply because we try to bypass this process.

Let's look in a bit more detail at the hawthorn. In Britain there are two species of hawthorn tree that are native, the common, and the midland hawthorn, which is more restricted in range. These species are similar and closely related, one of the main differences between the two being the number of seeds present in each berry. *Monogyna*, the second part of the scientific name of the common hawthorn, tells us precisely how many seeds each of its haws has – one – while the midland has two or three.

Dormancy in seeds is a form of insurance on the tree's part. It enables the seed to stay viable within its shell until conditions are suited to it germinating. In many trees this is light-related, especially within woodlands where the amount of light penetrating a fully closed canopy of leaves is minimal. If a hawthorn berry were to fall directly below its parent tree and land on the woodland floor, then when the leaves emerge on its parent and its parent's closely packed neighbours it would inevitably be in a shady location. Growing up in the shadow of a dominant parent is not easy. The flesh of many berries contains germination inhibitors – chemical compounds that reduce the chances of the seed within the berry germinating the following spring.

This makes sense. If a hawthorn berry, dislodged by a bird feeding on the neighbouring haws, drops straight down to the ground, it would be disadvantaged on germinating in the following spring, as it would be doing so in shade. Most trees need good sunlight to grow well, especially when they are small saplings striving to gain energy via photosynthesis to sustain their growth. A sapling in the shade of other trees is going to struggle, often terminally. (There are, as always, exceptions; some species are shade-tolerant, the common beech being a good example. It is a climatic tree, able to germinate and grow under other trees, before eventually outcompeting them, then remorselessly shading those trees out of existence.[67])

The woodland floor beneath its parents is not where a young hawthorn needs to be. The germination inhibitors in the flesh are only a temporary block – the berry flesh soon

---

67 This takes decades, even centuries, to happen, but just because trees are slower in their processes than we are, it doesn't mean they are not active. Woodlands are dynamic systems, not static ones as many people perceive them. The beech also suppresses competition further with chemical inhibitors in its leaves, which blanket the floor of beech woodland, stopping the germination of other species.

vanishes, either rotting away or consumed by invertebrates. But the seed case within the flesh is also a germination inhibitor, a solid wall keeping the potential young tree within, preventing it from breaking out. It does degrade over time, of course, but it does so slowly. In human terms, the seed is biding its time, awaiting a fortuitous opportunity. That fortuitous opportunity is usually the death of the tree above. If you walk through a woodland where a tree has either recently died or been removed, you should see a wealth of new growth pullulating upwards from the soil.[68] Tree seeds that have lain dormant in the shady conditions for long periods of time are suddenly able to take advantage of the light now able to reach the woodland floor. It is a strategy that doesn't always work – trees are long-lived – but that's the thing with insurance policies; most are never used.

The ideal germination conditions for a hawthorn seed are open unshaded ground, where the sun's warmth and light can reach it without obstruction. Exactly the sort of conditions you find in my raised vegetable bed. In these sorts of conditions the presence of any germination inhibitor would be a disadvantage; delaying emergence by a year or two would potentially allow other plants to become established, shading out the ground, and therefore the dormant seed, beneath. But a hawthorn berry can't just drop straight off the tree and land in open unshaded land like the veg bed; it has to be transported there. And in my case it's a blackbird that will have done it.

A blackbird providing this courier service first of all removes the flesh of the berry. It takes its payment, and as it does so it takes with it the inhibitors present. It then passes the seed through its gut. This passage might be quick, but it is long enough for damage to occur to the seed case. This damage is called scarification; the surface of the seed case gets scratched and worn by the digestive process, removing the inhibiting action. Therefore, come the spring, come the return of warmth and light, the seed is able to germinate in advantageous conditions. Birds don't just deliver the seeds – they process them too.

To be able to germinate quickly, many tree seeds that are encased in red berries need to pass through a bird's digestive process;[69] if they don't, it can negatively impact their chances of ever germinating. Most examples of this long-evolved mutually beneficial relationship between trees and birds are pretty generalised; the hawthorn tree doesn't rely on just the blackbird, but a variety of birds, to carry out the distribution and propagation process. This is the norm for trees, but it isn't always the case; some species of tree have grown dependent on just a few species of fruit-feeding birds. Narrowing options is always risky, though; putting all your eggs in one basket may work well, but if something upsets that basket all can be lost.

Nothing upsets baskets full of eggs like we humans do, and the most delicate baskets of all are to be found on remote islands.

---

68 Unfortunately, the unnaturally high deer pressure in the vast majority of the woodlands in Britain means that this process is rarely seen in its full glory.

69 This doesn't mean that they have to travel through the gut of the bird; some seeds get coughed up by the bird once the flesh has been stripped in the gullet, and this has a similar effect on the seed within.

A delicate balance

The western Pacific island of Guam is officially described as an Unincorporated Territory of the United States of America – a bit of a mouthful for an island that lies within the geographical region of Micronesia, a region that has thousands of small islands, of which, at around 212 square miles, it is the largest. Guam has a tropical rainforest climate, but humans first colonised it over 3,500 years ago, and so the extent of natural occurring forest has inevitably been greatly reduced. It is now more tropical rain forest in climate than in habitat.

Around 70 per cent of all the tree species native to Guam have evolved a mutualistic relationship with the native birds of the island for their seed distribution. The fruits of these trees attract the birds, and the birds, feeding on them, disperse the seeds they hold within them in just the same way as the blackbird in my garden does for the hawthorn.

Despite the long history of human settlement on the island, these relationships remained pretty much intact until relatively recently. In World War II, Guam was invaded and captured by the Japanese in late 1941;[70] it was another two and half years before the Americans were able to recapture it. Following the recapture, the Americans imported a vast quantity of supplies to help rebuild the island's infrastructure, which had been badly damaged in the lengthy and devastating battle to retake it. Unfortunately for the island's ecology, one, or most probably some, of these imports came with some stowaways. One of these was the brown tree snake.

This is a nocturnal tree-climbing snake found naturally in parts of Australia, Papua New Guinea and Indonesia. Within its natural range it is a pretty unremarkable component of the ecosystem, growing to around 1–2 metres in length, and feeding on a wide variety of prey such as birds, bats, lizards and small rodents. In its native range it is not top of the food chain, and is predated on by a number of other species, including other snakes.

But Guam is not in its natural range, and on this island the snake has no natural predators. No natural checks are present to maintain that all-important and long-evolved balance between predator and prey. The island's highly specialised bird life had never encountered a tree-climbing nocturnal predator like the brown tree snake before; the birds had no experience in dealing with such a thing, so were incredibly vulnerable to it. Because of the lack of predators, the abundance of potentially easily caught prey and a climate that enabled the snake to reproduce throughout the year, it has been incredibly successful in its new island home, reaching densities of 100 snakes per hectare in some places.

The snake may have been successful in its new home, but its success has had a devastating impact on the bird life of the island. Before the snake's human-assisted arrival there were 12 native bird species that inhabited the remaining forests of the island, and many of these birds, like the rather beautiful Mariana fruit dove, were fruit feeders. Ten of these species have been wiped out on the island, and the remaining two have the dubious accolade of

---

70 The same day as the US fleet at Pearl Harbor was attacked: 8 December 1941.

being described as functionally extinct. The entire forest avifauna of Guam has been wiped out because of our, albeit accidental, careless introduction of this snake. We have turned a once vibrant ecosystem into what is now described heartbreakingly as a silent forest.

But the snake's introduction hasn't affected the birds alone. As the birds have gone, the unique relationships between them and the other species of flora and fauna on the island have gone too. If 70 per cent of the island's trees used birds as their fruit-dispersal mechanism, the loss of the birds means that 70 per cent of the island's trees have lost their seed propagators.

What does this mean for the remaining forests of Guam? Trees are of course long-lived, so the full impact of our carelessness will take time to come to fruition, if you'll pardon the pun – but already, just a few decades after the introduction of the brown tree snake, profound changes are being discovered. As we have seen, birds carry out two roles in their seed dispersal. First they prepare the seed for germination by cleansing it of its fleshy fruit surround and by scarifying the hard seed case, the endocarp. Then they move the seeds away from the parent tree, an important action, as in most rainforests across the world seedlings germinate more successfully when they are not in the immediate vicinity of their own kind.[71]

With such a high number of tree species in the forests of Guam using birds as their seed dispersal mechanism, it could be said that the layout of those forests, the actual distribution of tree species within them, was determined by the birds. For millennia the birds were in effect landscape architects. But now these natural landscape designers are gone. Studies of the forests on Guam have shown that without the birds the seeds of fruit-bearing trees are now almost entirely falling to the ground directly underneath their parent tree – and this, combined with them not having passed through the avian digestive system, had led to up to a 92 per cent decline in seedling recruitment.[72]

In this respect 92 per cent is a scarily high number; the knock-on effects of the introduction of the brown tree snake has effectively neutered many of the native component tree species of an entire island's forest ecosystem. The snake's presence has wiped out not just the birds – it is changing the very make-up of the forest. The number of fruit-bearing trees within those forests is destined to decline drastically, and the very few that do make it to maturity will not be evenly spread across the habitat, as they were before. It is very easy to look at the introduction of the brown tree snake as being utterly disastrous for the native birds of Guam; they are, if you like, the poster boys of this human-induced ecological cockup. But it is disastrous, too, for many of the native tree species. And the disaster won't stop with them – there will be countless species of invertebrates, fungi, bryophytes etc that will have developed ecological relationships with the trees that are now no longer producing

---

71 This could be for a variety of reasons, including distancing themselves from pests and pathogens that may be in high numbers around existing specimens of the species.

72 Data taken from a fascinating and excellent paper: Rogers, H.S. et al. 'Effects of an Invasive Predator Cascade to Plants via Mutualism Disruption'. *Nat. Commun.* 8, 14557 doi: 10.1038/ncomms14557 (2017).

viable numbers of new specimens. They too will bear the brunt of our carelessness.

Humans wreaking havoc with island ecosystems is nothing new, of course; perhaps the most notorious example of this happened a few centuries earlier.

As dead as a dodo

If you ask someone to name an extinct species, it is highly likely that they will name the dodo, the infamously famous flightless pigeon[73] that once graced the beautiful island of Mauritius in the Indian Ocean. This iconic bird became extinct in around 1662, just 64 years after humans settled on the island and first recorded the bird's existence. Since its extremely rapid demise, the dodo has become a synonym for death, failure and obsolescence. Its extinction has become a cliché that masks the real tragedy of what we humans did just a few centuries ago. We even use the bird's name as an insult, using it to refer to someone's stupidity, the idea being that the bird was so stupid that it was easily rendered extinct. In other words, it wasn't our fault, it was the bird's. This is a classic example of the all-too-human trait of shifting the blame onto the victim.

But the dodo wasn't stupid – after all, that is solely a human trait – it was in fact a bird perfectly adapted to its isolated island environment, honed by evolution to successfully exploit a niche. Flightlessness is not overly unusual in the avian world – penguins being the classic example – even though when we think of birds we tend to think of flight. It is a trait that probably evolved around the time of the mass extinction event 66 million years ago, which led to the demise of the non-avian dinosaurs. Mass extinctions are by their very nature terrible events – but they also, quite literally, open up a whole world of opportunities for the forms of life that survive them. The avian dinosaurs that survived found themselves in a world full of unexploited niches. Nature abhors a vacuum, as the saying goes, and evolution never rests.

A mistake often made is the concept that the birds that fly evolved from the birds that don't – that birds such as the penguin and the ostrich are the precursors to birds such as the puffin and the bustard. But this is not the case. In fact it's the opposite way around: flightless birds evolved from flying ones. And they have done so countless times throughout the last 66 million years. Over that time, many species have come and gone throughout the whole sphere of flora and fauna, but flightlessness in birds has persisted, although now, with the dominance of the mammals, the number of bird species that exhibit that trait has waned considerably.

Even so, in the current geological era, the Holocene, there are still around 200 species of flightless birds. Or rather, there should be. Those 200 have been ruthlessly pared down to

---

73 A relation of the ill-fated Marian fruit dove that inhabited Guam. Pigeons are common birds, but many species of them – including the passenger pigeon of North America, blasted out of the skies by stupidity and greed – have become extinct in the last few centuries because of humanity's actions.

around just 60 species. The cause of this massive reduction? Invariably, it is humans. There may be a case to be made for an extreme weather event – a hurricane, for example – being responsible for wiping out a geographically limited bird species or two, but the harsh reality is, it us humans that are responsible for the vast majority of extinctions in the Holocene.

Most of the flightless birds that have gone forever had inhabited remote islands, long separated from large landmasses and therefore devoid of mammalian predators. These islands had the right niches available for flightlessness to evolve, and so it did; it was only when humans blundered onto the scene that flightlessness become a serious evolutionary disadvantage.

Mauritius is part of the Mascarene Islands, an isolated archipelago surrounded by vast expanses of ocean and separated from the largest land mass (Madagascar) by between 700 and 1,500 kms. These small islands, lacking land mammals, had evolved a number of endemic flightless birds, but in the last few hundred years they have all become extinct. Not just the dodo, but at least 13 other flightless species[74] from this remote island chain have become mere footnotes in the pages of our history.

It is not necessarily humans *per se* that are the problem; as we saw in the previous chapter it is often what humans bring that causes the most damage. Whilst dodos were indeed hunted by sailors for food, it is now widely thought that it was the mammals that humans introduced to the island that were the key factors leading to the bird's extinction. Rats may have played a part, but the pigs and macaques that were deliberately introduced would have been absolutely devastating to a ground-nesting bird with no defence against them. In just a few decades the dodo, and many other unique species of flora and fauna, were gone forever.

Today the island of Mauritius is still an amazing place, and whilst its wide range of endemic species of both flora and fauna has been severely depleted, it still has some species found nowhere else on the planet. One of these endemic species that has survived our ravages – although it is still regarded as endangered – is the tambalacoque tree. The tall tambalacoque belongs to a large family of tree species that are tropical in their distribution. Yet the family sits within the order Ericales, which means that this tree, although endemic to Mauritius, is related to species more familiar to us such as rhododendrons, heathers and the blueberry.

In 1973 it was announced to the world by Stanley Temple of the University of Wisconsin that there were only 13 examples of this tree left, and that all of the unlucky few were over 300 years old; there were no younger trees to be found, no new saplings forthcoming. It seemed as if the tambalacoque tree was about to follow the dodo out of the exit door. But why was this tree heading for extinction? Temple hypothesised that the tambalacoque had formed an obligate plant–animal mutualism with the dodo, and that without the bird the tree was inevitably doomed. It was functionally extinct.

In 1977 Temple published a headline-grabbing scientific paper in the world-renowned

74 Including the Rodrigues solitaire, yet another species of pigeon.

magazine *Science*, entitled 'Plant–Animal Mutualism: Coevolution with Dodo leads to Near Extinction of Plant'.[75] It was sensational stuff. Anything to do with the dodo is bound to catch people's attention, and so this paper did, widely quoted not just in the scientific press but also in the popular media at the time, and regurgitated endlessly in books afterwards.

To summarise Temple's theory, the fruits of the tambalacoque are encased in a hard endocarp.[76] For these seeds to germinate this endocarp has to be abraded or scarified, worn down by some mechanism or other. The mechanism for doing that was, according to the theory, the digestive tract of the now long-dead dodo. Temple argued that the reason why the only remaining tambalacoques were all over 300 years old was that the dodo had become extinct around 300 years before, and when the bird went so too did the only mechanism for abrading the tree's hard seed case. If there was no dodo to eat the seeds, there would be no germination.

It was an appealing theory, and one that seemed to make instant sense. At the time the idea that wildlife existed in the networks that we call ecosystems was beginning to gain traction with the wider public. What a great example, then, of how our actions directly impact not just one species, but other species that coexist with the first. To make the theory even more appealing, especially to the mass media, there was a potential happy ending to the paper. In order to help demonstrate his theory, Temple, using captive turkeys as a dodo substitute, had force-fed them the seeds of the tambalacoque. He was able to show that after passing through the bird's digestive system some of these seeds germinated – the dodo may have been long gone, but the tree could be saved after all!

It may have been an appealing theory, it may have seemed to make perfect sense – but almost immediately the theory that tree and bird were inextricably linked was vociferously questioned by the scientific community, who immediately cited a whole host of evidence that the theory was wrong. This evidence included the fact that a paper published in 1941 had shown that the seeds of the tambalacoque germinated without the need for abrading, that the number of tambalacoques growing on the island was actually in the hundreds, and that many of these trees were significantly younger than 300 years. The attractive theory of an obligate mutualistic existence between the dodo and the tambalacoque had been blown out of the water.

Or rather, it should have been. Even though a number of follow-up papers also disproved Temple's theory, none of them apparently reached the wider public's consciousness, and none of them captured the public's imagination as the original paper had so dramatically done. The mainstream media were no longer interested in the story; it had been and gone, the headlines had been printed, the story read; the media had moved on to the next sensation, uninterested in revisiting an old one.

---

75 S. Temple. 'Plant-Animal Mutualism: Coevolution with Dodo leads to Near Extinction of Plant'. *Science* magazine vol. 197, issue 4306 DOI: 10.1126/science.197.4306.885

76 The shell of an almond is a good example,

A major factor in the ignoring of the follow-up publications that countered the theory was that Temple's original paper hadn't been published in an obscure scientific journal, but in one of the most prestigious and highly regarded science publications there is, *Science*. This had given it tremendous kudos and ensured that even if the vast majority of people had never read the paper they would have heard about it. To the public at large, the theory of the dodo and the tambalacoque living in a perfect harmony had become a fact, even though it was actually a factoid.[77] And this was a factoid that was very, very persistent. It was widely repeated in book after book, article after article[78] – and, later on, website after website. It can still be found as an absolute on many websites today, over four decades later; a search for dodo and tambalacoque tree will soon find examples.

In 2004 *Plant Science Bulletin*, the journal of the Botanical Society of America, published a fabulously damning paper on 'the Dodo–Tambalacoque myth'. The paper, written by David R. Hershey, was entitled 'The Widespread Misconception that the Tambalacoque or Calvaria Tree Absolutely Required the Dodo Bird for its Seeds to Germinate.'[79] It is a great example of how to dismantle a theory, and is well worth a read in full.

Following that paper and the many others that not only contradicted Temple's original paper but also heavily criticised his methods, it is no longer accepted that the dodo and the tambalacoque were an example of an obligate mutualistic interaction between bird and tree. It is, of course, highly likely that the dodo *did* feed on the tree's fleshy fruits and probably did pass the seeds through its gut, and that by doing so it would have indeed helped disperse the seeds – but it wasn't the only animal to do so. Hershey was happy to acknowledge that the dodo had played a role in the dispersal of the seeds of the tambalacoque tree. He had no argument with this. His argument was with the perceived exclusivity of this relationship, that without the dodo the tree couldn't successfully set seed.

Despite Hershey's brilliantly written paper, the original theory still continues to be widely believed and disseminated. This isn't because those who believe it refuse to accept the arguments of scientists like Hershey; it is because those arguments just don't get heard by the wider audience. I don't know where I first heard about the dodo and the tambalacoque tree, but what I do know is that the theory that the tree needed the extinct bird found its way into my brain as a fact, and stuck there. I never questioned it; after all, to me it just seemed so possible, so right. I know that species don't exist as individuals, but as part of an interconnected web of life, that they interact with other species, often passively, and that the interaction, no matter how small, can be vital to the continued health of an ecosystem.

---

77 A term coined by the American writer Norman Mailer that refers to something that looks very much like a fact, but in actual fact isn't.

78 I hold my hand up at this point and admit that I too in the past have repeated the factoid, thinking it was a fact.

79 D.R. Hershey. 'The Widespread Misconception that the Tambalacoque or Calvaria Tree Absolutely Required the Dodo Bird for its Seeds to Germinate'. *Plant Science Bulletin* 50. 2004.

I know too that removing one species will have an effect on the others in that system. This seemed to be the perfect example. But now I know it wasn't. Temple's theory is … well, how else can I put it? It's as dead as a dodo.

For me, the saddest thing is that whilst Temple was coming up with his theory, and whilst Hershey and others were refuting it, the ecological disaster of Guam was playing out before our very eyes. Some of the trees of Guam, like some of the trees of Mauritius, depend on birds to distribute their seeds; it might not be an exclusive relationship, with just one species of bird, but it exists nonetheless. The tambalacoque had most probably lost an important disperser of its seed when the dodo became extinct, but it had other mechanisms available to it, some of which have been introduced by us. But in Guam, it wasn't just one species of native bird that became extinct – it was *all* of them. That impact is something that we are only just beginning to appreciate.

Out of place down under

When we remove a species from an ecosystem it has consequences, but when we introduce a species there are consequences as well.

Humans have a long history of removing species from the naturally evolved ecosystems in which they live, causing local extinctions – and, more finally, worldwide extinctions. We have been the cause, one way or another of far too many bird extinctions: the dodo, the passenger pigeon, the great auk … The list of the known extinctions alone is a long one; nearly 200 birds as a result of our actions since 1500. But we don't just take, we also give. And our presents can be unwelcome.

At one stage in our recent history, despite the fact that the British Isles make up just 0.16 per cent of the world's land area, Britain laid claim to 24 per cent of that area. We were everywhere; we had our men and women posted throughout the world. The sun, famously, never set on our empire.

In many places, to help the good servants of the Crown get used to their strange surroundings, the British came up with the idea of introducing familiar species of wildlife to live alongside these people, helping them feel more at home. We formed acclimatisation societies to do this, to bring a bit of Britain along to enrich what, in our usual arrogant way, we had decided were impoverished territories, lacking natural flora and fauna. The British knew best when it came to telling a quarter of the world's human population how to live their lives, and we were in no doubt that our own wildlife was also the best option for many of these places.

It was during the Victorian era that those societies were formed; we even formed one for Britain itself, with, amongst many unsuitable species, the large African antelope, the eland, being proposed for introduction to the British Isles, principally based on the opinion that it was good to eat.[80] But it was in Australia and New Zealand in the 1860s that the acclimatisation societies achieved their zenith. Or should that be nadir?

Australia and New Zealand were part of a land mass that broke away from the Gondwana[81] land mass between 130 and 85 million years ago. By the time of the meteorite strike 66 million years ago the land mass that would become New Zealand had already separated from Australia. These landmasses have existed in isolation ever since – an isolation that has led to their own distinct floras and faunas evolving; this is why creatures such as platypuses, kangaroos and kiwis are so unique in appearance and behaviour.

But these unique and special floras and faunas weren't good enough for the British colonists. In their minds these species needed to be improved, to be made better, to be made more *British*. They went about doing so without any consideration of scientific knowledge, without any thought at all as to the consequences of their actions. What they achieved was disastrous in the extreme. Looking at the list of species that British colonists introduced to these countries is like reading through a litany of ecological catastrophes.

The list is long, but for the purposes of this book we are going to focus on just two species, the first of which is the blackbird.

As we have already discussed, blackbirds are excellent dispersers of tree seed; it is a key part of their ecological role. If a tree in Britain has a red fruit it is extremely likely that the blackbird helps propagate it. In the 1850s blackbirds were first introduced privately to Australia, and there followed a succession of larger-scale introductions, especially in the 1860s after the formation of several of the aforementioned acclimatisation societies. In Britain we view the birds as a benign and beautiful garden bird, one that can give us the opportunity to see it at close quarters as it hops across our lawns. In Australia, however, the view is somewhat different; here it is a pest species, with risk assessments drawn up and management strategies in place.

It is the same for the second species we will look at: the common hawthorn. Introducing a non-native pioneer species of tree and its equally non-native seed dispersal system into a unique ecosystem was never going to be a good idea.

The exact date when the hawthorn was introduced to Australia isn't known. It was introduced as a hedging plant, a traditional use for it in Britain, to help the colonists keep their newly introduced sheep under control. It is now found growing as an 'invasive weed' (as it seems to be known in virtually every Australian local government document I have read) in the south and east of the country, where it is liable to invade natural forests, woods and riparian habitats, shading out natural species and inhibiting the growth of native trees. It also plays host to 'undesirable birds', a phrase those documents use to describe blackbirds.

---

80 And yes it was tried; see the book *They Dined on Eland* by Christopher Lever for a full account of this and other examples.

81 Gondwana was a supercontinent; it also contained the land masses of what today are South America, Africa, Antarctica, the Indian subcontinent and Arabia.

Australia is split politically into states which have their own legislative assemblies; each state is responsible for its own laws and management policies, and these policies dictate how the hawthorn is viewed. In the state of Victoria, the hawthorn is listed as being a regionally controlled weed, landowners having to take all reasonable steps to control it and prevent its spread on their land. In the Australian Capital Territory (a small state around Canberra) the hawthorn is described as a pest plant that must be contained; its propagation and supply is prohibited. In Western Australia it is listed as 'prohibited', and it is not permitted entry into the state.

Of course, refusing entry to a tree at a state border isn't as simple as it seems, especially one that spreads with the help of birds, so it is important that the state's neighbour, South Australia,[82] helps – and it does, for there, this beautiful British native tree is declared a noxious weed that needs urgent removal when it is detected.

The blackbird is treated as a pest species because of its role in the spread of the hawthorn, but it is not just this tree that it spreads; many more species of plants were introduced to the antipodes by us, and many of them are now declared to be invasive weeds which seriously threaten native flora and associated natural habitats. Amongst these are plants very familiar to us in Britain, including bramble and ivy, both of which are readily spread by the fruit-eating habits of the blackbird. But there are others from other parts of the world too, pyracantha and cotoneaster, for example. They too are now listed as invasive weeds, and they too produce the red berries that blackbirds love to feed on.

Blackbird in Australia

---

82 Western Australia's other neighbouring state is the Northern Territory, but it's outwith the blackbird's range.

The blackbird is just doing what is natural to it; participating in a mutually beneficial symbiotic relationship that evolved long ago. It is not the bird's fault that this is now playing out at the opposite end of the world from where it should be happening. It is our fault – entirely our fault – but it is the blackbird that bears the brunt of our mistakes. In the south-east of the country the bird is now so well established that co-ordinated control methods[83] are only used when the bird is perceived to be a commercial pest in orchards or vineyards. But it has no legal protection, and can be shot or trapped with impunity by anyone.

In Western Australia the blackbird is listed as Absent, and the state government is determined that it should stay that way. Legally it is listed as an organism that is excluded from existing in all parts of the state. In purely layman terms, blackbirds are shot on sight.

Anyone who knows me will know I have a very big soft spot for these beautiful members of the thrush family. As I write this, during a cold snap in the winter, I am constantly being distracted by 'our' male blackbird, a bird that has somehow managed to train us to provide it with mealworms and suet pellets when it wants them, coming to a perch by the window to attract our attention. We love having this wild bird interact with us in this way – it brings us tremendous joy. You would think therefore that the thought of blackbirds being shot on sight would be complete anathema to me.

Indeed it is – but I can understand the reasons why such drastic action is taken. The native, often endemic, flora and fauna of Australia have been hit badly since the British colonisers arrived in 1788. Since then at least 51 species of bird and mammal have become extinct. It is believed that one of the causes for the extinction of one of those birds, the Tasman starling, was competition with the introduced blackbird. Alongside the extinctions there has also been a widespread degradation of the native habitats of the country – unique ecosystems that have been badly damaged, if not wrecked, by us and our careless activities, of which introductions of non-native species play a significant part.

Hawthorn, ivy and bramble have caused, and still can cause, serious damage to native habitats, altering the structure of the habitat and putting native species of both plant and animal under serious threat. Blackbirds are, unfortunately, very good at spreading these plants, which is no surprise because it is part of their role in an ecosystem; but, sadly, both they and the plants they spread are in the wrong ecosystem. They shouldn't be anywhere near Australia. What is left of the highly fragmented and damaged native habitats of the country need protection.

In Australia's neighbour, New Zealand, the tale is similar but subtly different. New Zealand was 'discovered' by Europeans in the 1600s and was regularly used and visited by them in the years that followed, Britain formally declaring its ownership of the country in 1840. The New Zealand landmass is so remote that it was the last large area of land to be colonised by humans; this had occurred when Polynesian travellers discovered it sometime between 1250 and 1300. Before they arrived, the only mammals that New Zealand had

---

83 Killing.

were a few bats and numerous species of whale, dolphin and seal. There were no terrestrial mammals. That soon changed.

The Polynesian settlers, who would become known as Maoris, brought with them dogs and rats,[84] mammalian predators that have a long and well-documented history of wreaking havoc on island species. But it wasn't just these animals that had an impact on the islands' flora and fauna. The people themselves had a drastic impact. It has been estimated that at the time the first humans arrived in New Zealand 80 per cent of it was covered by forest, but by the time the Europeans arrived that was down to just 40 per cent. Those first human settlers had probably reduced the forest cover, the unique forest cover, by half.

Because of the long period of isolation from any other landmass, the flora and fauna of New Zealand is very different from those of anywhere else on the planet. The lack of terrestrial mammals saw a large number of flightless birds evolve, and these species would suffer greatly when mammals, in the form of humans, finally got there. In the period between the arrival of the Polynesians and the arrival of the Europeans, at least 23 species of bird (both flighted and flightless) became extinct, including the huge moas and their predator, one of the world's largest ever raptors, the Haast's eagle. Impressive birds gone forever, leaving only their bones as evidence of their existence. It didn't get better after the Europeans arrived; in fact it got worse.

Since the 19th century the forest cover of the islands has dropped further; it is now around 23 per cent of the original. And with the increase in people and the inevitable animals they brought with them, including domestic cats and pigs, the number of bird species pushed beyond the brink went up as well; a further 22 species became extinct. Between them, the two different waves of human settlers have reduced the forest cover of the islands to a little over a quarter of what it once was; they have also extirpated at least 55 species of bird.

In a mirror image of what happened in Australia, the British colonisers decided to form acclimatisation societies and introduce species that really shouldn't be there. The New Zealand acclimatisation societies, duly formed, introduced a wide variety of plants, fish, mammals and birds, including the blackbird.

The blackbird is one of the commonest birds in New Zealand. It is certainly the most widespread, and is, along with the native silvereye,[85] the main disperser of tree fruit seed, and therefore effectively the main manager of fruit-bearing plant communities in the country. Just as in Australia, humans introduced species such as hawthorn, bramble, ivy and rowan, and these, with the skills of the blackbird, are now widely established plants on the islands, outcompeting native plant communities and altering habitats.

---

84 The Polynesian rat, the third most widespread rat species in the world after the brown and black.

85 The silvereye is what is known as a self-introduced species, a bit like the collared dove in Britain. Silvereyes first turned up in the mid-1800s, when a migrating flock from Australia was blown off course by a storm.

So far, this sounds exactly like what had happened in Australia, but the difference here is that New Zealand has what has been described as a 'wreckage of an avifauna'; although Australia's native species have suffered, they haven't suffered anywhere near as badly as New Zealand's. Since humans arrived, New Zealand has lost almost half of its native (and often endemic) bird species. Some of these long-gone birds were fruit-feeding seed dispersers, and when they became extinct the native trees and plants lost their principal means of dispersing and propagating their seeds. It is just what has happened in Guam in more recent times, the important difference being that New Zealand now has an avian substitute on the field of play.

The blackbird is a non-native invasive species, and it has created large areas of non-native plant communities dominated by hawthorn, rowan etc. It has had a negative impact. But because of the blackbird's innate habits and the lack of the species that should be present, it is one of the principal dispersers and propagators of native seed as well. So the presence of blackbirds has positive effects as well as negative ones. Unlike in Australia, there are no shoot-on-sight policies, no risk assessments or management plans; the blackbird has filled an ecological vacuum created by us, and in doing so it is both causing and solving problems.

Now we'll leave the theatre of introduced species to isolated islands and look a bit more closely at an isolated island environment that is still pretty much intact – one where the relationship between birds and trees isn't just about dispersing the seed, but also about creating it in the first place.

A holy alliance

The process of birds eating berries and subsequently dispersing the seeds is probably the most widely known example of mutualistic relationships between trees and birds. As mentioned earlier, birds that are pollinators of trees are less widely known, but when we think about it, the images of hummingbirds busying themselves around tropical tree flowers are ones we know well. So while some birds pollinate, others disperse seeds. But are there birds that carry out pollination of a tree and then distribute the resulting seeds? A double mutualistic relationship?

Yes, there are. Actually there are quite a few; they are generally restricted to isolated island chains where the overall diversity of life has been geographically limited. As a result of this isolation the birds' diversity is often more extensive than might otherwise be the case. The species present have often evolved to fulfil a variety of roles that would otherwise have been filled by other species. Birds, very mobile creatures, are able to colonise these isolated islands, islands replete with vacant ecological niches; it is then down to time and evolution to do the rest.

Species that both pollinate trees and then distribute the seeds are known as dual mutualists. But it is possible to go one step further; there are some triple mutualists.

The Galápagos flycatcher is a small member of the wonderfully named family, tyrant flycatchers.[86] This very large family is the Americas' version of the old world flycatchers, two groups of birds that despite similarities in the ways they are named, look and behave, are not in fact closely related to one another. Measuring around 15 cm in length and being a generally brownish-hued bird, the Galápagos flycatcher looks a lot like the spotted flycatcher found in Britain.

If you have ever visited the Galápagos Islands you will have most probably seen this bird. It doesn't seem bothered by humans, and will often use people as a perch, a handy spot from where they can do what their name suggests: catch flies. But these aren't just insect eaters; the wet and dry seasons of the islands they live on govern the availability of food for them, so they need to be adaptable in their diet in order to survive these somewhat boom-and-bust conditions.

This small, rather unobtrusively coloured bird has formed a mutually beneficial relationship with a tree that in the local language is called the *palo santo* – holy stick. This is a bit more than a stick, though; holy or not, it is an attractive small tree with very pale grey stems and shoots. It is a component of a habitat known as tropical dry forest, which unlike the more familiar tropical rainforest, is – well, you guessed it – pretty dry. But it's not completely dry; although it sounds counterintuitive it does rain in tropical dry forest, but unlike in the tropical rain forest, it only rains there for a short season. For many months of the year there is no rainfall whatsoever.

The *palo santo* can be found in these dry forests across Central America, from the Atlantic coasts of Mexico through to the Pacific coasts of Peru. It is also abundant on the Galápagos. The tree is in the same family as the trees that give us frankincense and myrrh, and this explains its common name; the very aromatic wood of this holy stick is widely used as incense in a variety of religious rituals, as is an oil decocted from it.

These trees only produce leaves in the wet season. In the dry season the leaves would lose too much moisture through transpiration, making them a liability, so once the rains stop the tree rapidly dispenses with its leaves. But during the relatively brief period that the tree bears them they are used to fuel the tree's growth, photosynthesis producing the carbohydrates the tree needs. During this verdant period the leaves, like so many leaves across the globe, are assailed by a whole host of leaf-eating insects and their larvae.

During the wet season in the Galápagos, insects abound, many species taking advantage of the moister climatic conditions to breed; the air can quite literally said to be abuzz with insects. This is of course a good thing if you are a flycatcher, and the Galápagos flycatcher takes advantage of this abundant life by timing its own breeding season to coincide with that of the insects. During this time the bird feeds on, and feeds its young on, a wide variety of insects, and some of those, whether as larvae or adults, feed on the leaves of the *palo santo*; they are defoliators that if unchecked could reduce the tree's capacity to produce the carbohydrates it needs. The flycatcher, and other bird species, provide that check.

---

86 A family of around 400 species, making them the largest bird family in the world.

This predation of defoliating invertebrates is the third string to the relationship's bow. The first string is pollination. Many of the animals on Galápagos feed on nectar, and the flycatcher is one of these. Before the beginning of the wet season the *palo santo* produces its flowers; they are relatively small, and they are white – not the red we associate with flowers pollinated by birds. But these flowers are not pollinated by birds alone. Lizards, on the wonderfully different world of the Galápagos, also act as pollinators. The flowers of this small tree have evolved to be as attractive to as many potential pollinators as they can possibly be.

Before the abundance of insects kicks in, the nectar in the tree's flowers is an important high-energy resource for the flycatcher. It may also help the bird get into breeding condition. Just as with the hummingbirds, sunbirds and honeyeaters we have looked at, the Galápagos flycatcher picks up pollen on its forehead as it feeds on the nectar inside the flower. The pollen is transferred to another flower when the bird feeds on its nectar. Once the blooms have been pollinated the nectar food source runs out – but by the time this happens the birds switch their diets and feed on the now-plentiful insects. But, again, only for a limited time, because as the wet season dries up, so does this food source.

Once the abundance of invertebrate prey drops below a certain level, most insect-eating birds would be forced to migrate to new areas, but the Galápagos flycatcher doesn't do this. Instead it switches diet again; it becomes a frugivore. With evolution-honed perfect timing, the flowers that the bird pollinated at the beginning of the wet season have now developed into fruits, and just as the wet season ends and the associated insects diminish in number, these fruits begin to ripen.

The fruits of the *palo santo* are small and round, and resemble miniature apples, in both colouration and shape. They have become an important food source for the flycatchers. The birds don't just feed on their flesh, though; they also swallow the seeds contained within them. The seeds are coated in lipids which act as a germination inhibitor, but the digestive system of the flycatcher is very effective at breaking these lipids down. The bird digests, and benefits from, the highly calorific fatty compounds, and the seeds benefit too, passing out through the bird minus their germination-inhibitor coating. So the Galápagos flycatchers are highly efficient processors of the *palo santo* seeds, and are highly efficient dispersers of them as well.

One scientific study noted that Galápagos flycatchers spend a lot of time perched in the branches of various small trees that are members of the Fabaceae family, such as the Galápagos acacia.[87] The birds inevitably defecate, depositing the *palo santo* seeds onto the ground directly below them. Members of the Fabaceae[88] family make excellent nurse plants

---

87 As mentioned in an earlier chapter, acacias have been reclassified taxonomically. The tree on the Galápagos is no longer technically an acacia, but the common name has stuck.

88 As we have already noted, the pea family or Fabaceae is a vast family of flowering plants. As well as the trees, it contains many important food crops such as beans and of course peas, not forgetting the beautiful and tiny little vetches that decorate our countryside in the spring and summer.

for other trees; they fix nitrogen in the soil, through specialised nodes on their root systems, which can then be used by the germinating plants as they grow. The established plants also shade these young germinators from excessive sunlight, helping them to avoid drying out – a major risk for young trees in the dry climate of this habitat. Many young trees – and the *palo santo* is one of them – have a higher survival rate if they grow beneath nurses such as these. So the flycatcher's habit of perching in the branches of the nurses is extremely beneficial to the *palo santo's* survival.

From these seeds, often deposited in just the right location, more holy sticks sprout. The more that sprout the more trees there will be in just a few years,[89] and more trees means more insects for the flycatchers to catch, as well as more flowers for them to feed on and pollinate. More pollinated flowers mean more fruits – fruits that will be produced just as the bird's insect food is waning. Thus more seeds will be consumed and processed by the bird's digestive system, leading to them being deposited beneath favourable nurses … And on it goes, in a positive feedback loop. When it comes to relationships between trees and birds, this is most a definitely a win-win-win one.

After that brief head-spinning trip around a positive feedback loop, allow me to take you on a different trip altogether: a trip into the world of intoxication.

Flying high

This might come as a surprise, but birds can get thoroughly drunk.[90] The sugars present in berries can ferment, especially after a bout of cold weather, and as birds feed on these fruits they consume the alcohol produced by the fermentation. Numerous studies have shown that bird species that feed on berries in the winter, like the beautiful waxwing, have evolved relatively large livers to help them break down the alcoholic content of fermented berries, but despite this adaptation some birds, especially younger ones, struggle to handle it.

In 2012 schoolchildren in the county of Cumbria discovered 12 dead blackbirds in their playground, and others that were acting very strangely. The police were called; staff were evidently worried that a possible poisoning had occurred, and there were real safety concerns. But following an examination by animal health officials the true reason behind the event was revealed. All of the dead birds had suffered major trauma injuries, injuries commensurate with flying into solid objects – solid objects such as school buildings. The post mortem also revealed a high alcohol content in the livers of the birds; they were drunk. Drink-flying is evidently a very dangerous thing to do. The dead birds were all recorded as being immature; they were in their first autumn and, as blackbirds often do, they had been feeding on a group of nearby rowan trees. Unfortunately for these young birds there had

---

89 *Palo santo* is a quick-growing and a quickly maturing tree.

90 Which I guess means that dinosaurs could get drunk; T-Rex on the town is an image that I find somewhat unnerving.

been a recent cold snap, a prolonged frost, and as a result the berries on the trees had started to ferment. One of the birds that didn't die was rescued after it was discovered staggering around the playground; it was taken to a wildlife rehabilitation centre where it propped itself up in its cage with its wings in much the same way as a drunk human will use their arms to hold themselves upright against a wall. After recovering from its rowan berry binge the bird was later released unharmed. It's not known if it had a headache.

There are many more examples of drunken behaviour in berry-eating birds, including redwings (a close relative of the blackbird) falling out of holly trees in various locations in Britain, whilst in Vienna it was reported that over 40 drunk birds flew into office windows. In some places this debauched deportment has led to the authorities getting involved, with the police in a town in Minnesota, USA, having to issue advice to human residents that they shouldn't be overly worried about the high number of drunk birds present in the town, saying that it was a just a temporary issue following an unseasonably early frost that had caused the berries to ferment.

Young blackbird

It seems that the vast majority of birds involved in these and many other cases are young and inexperienced ones. We've all been there. It is believed that adult birds may be able to develop some degree of tolerance to the alcohol over time, but importantly they also possess that wise quality of experience and have learnt to detect when berries have a high alcohol content. As a result they avoid selecting them, and opt instead to feed on berries that haven't fermented yet. If you watch a flock of birds feeding on berry-laden trees, you will soon notice that there is a distinct pecking order in operation; the adult birds will dominate the areas where the best food is available, and the younger birds are often pushed out, either having to wait their turn, if access to the food is limited, or moving to another food source. If the adults are deliberately avoiding berries with a high alcohol content, then these berries are likely to be the only ones available to the young birds, increasing the chances that the youngsters will consume one too many.

We only notice this when the birds get to a level of inebriation that noticeably affects their behaviour – usually, sadly, when they fly into buildings and the like – but it is likely that from time to time there are birds flying around that could well be described as a bit tipsy.

Birds getting drunk is likely to just be an incidental consequence of their diet – but might birds actively seek out intoxication, as some humans do? There is plenty of evidence showing that mammals do this: cats do it with catnip, reindeer reportedly do it with hallucinogenic mushrooms, bighorn sheep will take extraordinary risks to feed on a type of lichen that contains hallucinogens – and amazingly, even dolphins experiment with drugs.[91]

But do birds?

In his interesting and somewhat different book, *Intoxication*,[92] the late Ronald K. Siegel suggests that they do. It is a book that, as it says on the cover, challenges conventional wisdom. It is subtitled *The Universal Drive for Mind-Altering Substances*, and, having read it, I think I can say that the author knew his subject well. He states that all animals, be they humans, dolphins or birds, have four basic drives that govern their lives: hunger, thirst, sex and intoxication.

The toyon is a small tree native to the California hills. Like many trees it is a member of the rose family, and it is closely related to the apples. Despite its scientific placing, it is widely known as the California holly – even though it's completely unrelated to the hollies. The toyon tree gets its common name because its evergreen leaves are sharply toothed and it produces bright red berries that ripen in the run-up to Christmas, giving it its other common name, Christmas berry.

---

91 A BBC documentary filmed dolphins capturing the highly poisonous puffer fish and then carrying them around, gently, in their mouths. Puffer fish release a neurotoxin that can be deadly at high doses, but by treating them so gently the dolphins were only getting a small intoxicating dose. The dolphins were filmed deliberately seeking the puffer fish out, holding them in their mouths and then passing them carefully around to one another once they had received their own hit.

92 *Intoxication: the Universal Drive for Mind-Altering Substances*. Ronald K. Siegel, PhD. Published by Park Street Press, 2005.

It's an attractive tree, and the red berries certainly make it attractive to many species of bird who are the tree's seed dispersal agents – but are the birds getting more from the relationship than just a meal? Are the holly woods of the Californian hills an intoxicating magnet for them just as the Hollywood[93] of the Californian hills is for many humans?

The berries of the toyon contain a variety of chemical substances, and in the past these berries have traditionally been used by native Americans for various medicinal purposes, including pain relief. But there doesn't appear to be much evidence for them containing anything mind-altering, although some native American tribes did use the berries to make a form of cider.

In his book, Siegel documents a visit he made to an area of toyon trees growing near the small Californian city of Walnut Creek, an area that had a reputation for attracting large numbers of berry-eating birds, some of which would later exhibit signs of intoxication. The principal species he documents is the American robin – a bird that isn't a robin at all but a thrush, which of course makes it a close relative of the blackbird.[94]

He describes how he watched a few thousand birds descend onto a group of berry-laden toyon trees and how they then started to feed enthusiastically on the fruits. As he was watching them he began to note that small numbers of the birds were falling out of the trees and staggering around on the ground. After noting this behaviour increasing, he headed off in his car and noted several dead birds on the roadside that had evidently collided with vehicles; he also recorded finding others that had hit buildings. To me, it sounds as if he was describing thrushes that had one too many fermented berries – it sounds very similar to the behaviour previously mentioned – but Siegel was adamant that this was not the case. He stated that he had carried out a post-mortem on the dead birds, and that each one had a stomach full of toyon berries, but he also stated that he found no evidence of fermentation or alcohol during his examinations – although it is notable that he gave no details of how he looked, or checked, for either of those. It would also have been interesting to know how old the birds were that had died; were they inexperienced youngsters, I wonder? Again no mention of the bird's age was made.

Siegel was utterly convinced that the birds were deriving some form of mind-altering drug from the berries they were consuming, and whilst he was unsure if the birds found it a pleasant experience, he was also convinced that they didn't find it unpleasant. He went on to say that birds were driven (neatly tying in with his theory of four overarching drives) to consume intoxicating berries, but that they were saved from becoming addicts by seasonality; as the berries are available for only a short period of time, there was no possibility for them to continue their binge berrying.

---

93 Hollywood is supposedly not named after the abundance of Christmas holly that grows in the area, but it is certainly a big coincidence.

94 Many American birds have been labelled with names that recall European birds; as the American robin has a red breast, it is easy to see why early settlers likened the bird to the more familiar robin.

The book was first published in 1989, since then it has become widely accepted and widely reported – including almost yearly in the local newspapers that cover the Walnut Creek area – that young berry-eating birds are prone to a bit of overindulgence resulting in drunken behaviour, attributed to the alcoholic fermentation of some of the berries they are consuming. Despite Siegel's assertions, it would appear that the drugged, as opposed to drunk, theory doesn't hold much water with biologists and the wider public. But to be fair to Siegel, if someone had suggested in 1989 that dolphins seek out and then pass around puffer fish so that they can get a high, that person would have been laughed at. Yet today we know that this is true; mammals do indeed have a tendency to seek out mind-altering drugs. Whether it is a primary driver for us humans is debatable, but it does happen to some extent.

But birds aren't mammals, they are avian dinosaurs, and are very, very unrelated to us mammals. Their brains are very different from our mammalian ones, they think differently, quite literally. But you never know …

Berry abetting

Although the relationships between trees and birds are varied, and at times hard for us to label, there are none that we know of that fall under the category of 'parasitic'. However, birds do play a role in relationships with trees that are parasitic, the best known example being the one that involves that essential Christmas party ingredient, mistletoe. An example of a bird-and-berry interaction that is not beneficial to trees.

There are many species of mistletoe throughout the world[95] and, as is often the case, their taxonomy is somewhat unclear, especially as the name 'mistletoe' is widely used to refer to a range of plants that are only distantly related. But at least all of them do belong to the large biological order Santalales, named after the sandalwood trees, such as the Indian sandalwood, that provide extremely valuable timber and fragrant oils that are widely used in many religions. Like the mistletoe we know, these sandalwood trees are partially parasitic, taking some of the nutrients and all of the water they need to grow from other plants. Yes, trees can be parasites too.

The biological term for the mistletoe way of life is 'hemiparasitism';[96] the mistletoe gets only some of what it needs from its host, as opposed to everything. The common mistletoe that we see growing in Britain is a classic example of this hemiparasitic way of life; it grows on the stems of various trees, especially those species that have thin, rough bark such as the apple and hawthorn. The mistletoe uses its specialised roots, haustoria, to break through the tree's outer bark and interlace themselves into the tree's vascular system, from which it then steals the water and nutrients it requires. But as mistletoe has leaves it can also

---

95 Some studies suggest there may be as many as 1,500 species.

96 Meaning 'half-parasitism'.

photosynthesise, converting solar energy into carbohydrates that the plant can use to fuel its growth.

For mistletoes to find a suitable host tree, they need a helping hand – or, rather, a helping beak. Mistletoe berries are dangerously toxic to us mammals[97] but not to birds, and in a relationship that mirrors many of those that we have already covered, the plant employs the bird to deliver its seed, rewarding it with a berryful of food in the process.

The bird most associated with mistletoe in Britain is the bird named after it: the mistle thrush. This association doesn't stop with its common English name; the scientific name for the bird is *Turdus viscivorus*, 'mistletoe-eating thrush'. So it will come as no surprise to learn that during the winter months the bird does indeed eat the berries of the mistletoe, and is considered by many to be the main distributor of its seed in Britain. This, however is changing, but before we address that, let's look at this mistletoe-eating thrush.

The mistle thrush is found right across Europe; in Britain it is widespread, with a population of around 170,000 breeding pairs. It is a large and very upright-looking thrush, but it is less confiding in us than its relations, the song thrush and the blackbird and is generally rather wary of us humans. It can often be seen singing from the top of trees in the early spring, using the tree as a sound stage, broadcasting its blackbird-like song to assert its territorial rights and attract a mate. Like its relatives it eats invertebrates throughout the year, and in the winter, when these are harder to find, it feeds heavily on berries. But in feeding on the berries of the mistletoe it is unusual. Most birds either ignore or avoid these white fruits – after all the colour is not known to be attractive to birds – but the mistle thrush doesn't seem to mind it; in fact it seems to be positively attracted to the small round white fruits.

I grew up with the thought well and truly planted in my head that as the mistle thrush eats the berries, the sticky flesh of the fruit sticks to the bird's bill, resulting in the bird having to wipe it off on the rough bark of the tree, neatly depositing the seed as it does so in the perfect place for it to germinate. But in fact the mistle thrush nearly always eats the mistletoe berry whole, carefully plucking it off the plant and swallowing it, seed and all – a neat way to avoid getting the berry flesh stuck all over its bill, therefore negating the need for the bird to wipe its bill. Mistletoe berries are so sticky, though, that even the trip through the thrush's digestive system doesn't remove their stickiness, and when the seed passes out the other end it does so in a gooey sticky slime that adheres to whatever it lands on. As we have seen, the transit through a bird's gut is relatively quick, but in the time it takes the seed to pass through, the bird will have most likely moved on from where it was feeding, making the seed deposition a somewhat random affair. Whilst most tree seeds wrapped in a berry can germinate in many situations, those of the mistletoe can only germinate successfully if the seed is nestled nicely into a furrow or crack in the bark of the right sort of tree. If the

---

97 It has always intrigued me that a plant that our folklore associates with fertility is likely to kill you if you eat it. Surely this is the ultimate opposite of fertility?

thrush deposits the seed on a lawn whilst looking for worms, it is obviously not going to be able to germinate, but even if the bird does defecate in the right type of tree, the seed is most likely to drop through the branches to the ground below or end up suspended in a sticky slimy sac hanging from a twig. So the chances of a mistletoe seed eaten by a mistle thrush being deposited in a propitious spot on a tree's bark are very slim indeed.

Mistletoe has always had a somewhat patchy distribution in Britain. Its stronghold has long been the south-west Midlands, where it can be a relatively common plant, but elsewhere in England, despite it being recorded in most counties, it is generally only found in a few scattered localities. When I was younger, it wasn't something I noticed that often in Devon, other than in a group of trees alongside the M5 that were festooned with the plant. But in recent years, I have noticed more and more mistletoe in my home county, and in some places it has become a relatively common sight. This could be because I have become a bit more tuned into it – maybe I look a bit harder for mistletoe now – but it could also be that what I am actually noticing is a real change in its distribution and frequency. Or perhaps both.

In other countries in Europe such as France, where mistletoe is much more abundant, its main vector for dispersal isn't the mistle thrush, but the humble, yet rather natty, blackcap. This small warbler is a much more efficient courier for the sticky seeds of the mistletoe, and in the parts of the continent where the blackcap is resident all year around, the mistletoe's occurrence is much more regular than elsewhere. Blackcaps seek out and feed on the berries just as the mistle thrush does, but unlike this bigger bird, which is able to swallow the berry whole the blackcap doesn't swallow the seed; it only eats the flesh.

Blackcap

Instead, the seed, which is sticky as well, gets stuck to the bird's bill in exactly the manner that I had always believed happened with the mistle thrush, and to remove it the blackcap obligingly rubs its bill against the rough bark of the tree, usually leaving the seed in contact with the bark. There it can germinate, sending its haustoria into the tree to seek out the water and nutrients it needs. While it may take up to 30 minutes for the mistletoe seed to pass through the mistle thrush's digestive tract, the blackcap wipes its bill straight away, often choosing a piece of exposed bark very close to the original plant. This is why you will often find a tree adorned with several mistletoe plants close together, while a neighbouring tree of the same species may have none.

The blackcap of course occurs in Britain as well, but as it's a spring and summer visitor to our shores its visits don't coincide with the mistletoe berry season. But times are a-changing, and the bird is now becoming a much more common sight throughout the year in all parts of Britain. This is a bird that is changing its distribution, and as a result of this change, it is a bird that is now feeding on mistletoe berries in Britain.

But the blackcaps wintering in our country aren't necessarily the blackcaps breeding here. Studies have shown that our breeding birds are continuing their migration south, generally taking their winters around the Mediterranean coast, especially in southern Spain. So where are the birds wintering here coming from? It would appear that many of them are arriving from central Europe, from Germany and Poland, countries that have a much colder winter than we do; these continental blackcaps seem to have switched from wintering in southern Europe to wintering in Britain. Whilst our winter climate is undoubtedly milder than that of central Europe, it is still cold compared to the winters of places like southern Spain, so something must have influenced this switch in migratory behaviour.

Britain might not have Mediterranean winters, but it does have a bit of an obsession with bird food. The British spend £250 million on bird food every single year, supplying an estimated 150,000 tonnes of nutritious delights to the birds that feed in our gardens. Most of this food is provided in the winter months, and we know from various surveys that wintering blackcaps readily exploit this bonanza. It is thought that the food provided in gardens enables them not only to survive, but also to return to their central European breeding grounds a week or two ahead of birds that have wintered in the warmer south of continent. So it gives our overwintering blackcaps an advantage. By returning to their breeding grounds early, they can establish territories in the prime areas before potential rivals return from the Mediterranean; this in turn will probably lead to 'our' blackcaps producing more surviving young than those other birds. It is then highly probable that these young will follow the migratory behaviour of their parents and head to Britain to winter. This is changing the dynamics of the central European population; in a short space of time, the switch from the bird's traditional wintering grounds has become the norm for the majority of these blackcaps.

Interestingly, though, it has now been discovered that some of our wintering blackcaps come from birds that breed in northern Spain; they are eschewing the country that our own breeders head for so that they can exploit our bird tables. This surprising data has come about from recent ringing studies, showing how much we can still learn by looking harder at the birds we are seeing.

Wherever our wintering blackcaps originate from, it does seem as if they are responsible for the increase in mistletoe that we have seen in recent years. More wintering blackcaps in areas where mistletoe is present is going to lead to more highly efficient seed dispersal for the parasite, which means that there will be more trees suffering from the mistletoe's nutrient-nicking habits. Climate change is no doubt helping the blackcaps survive in Britain, but the ready availability of food in our gardens is probably the major driver behind their successful overwintering.

Whilst the blackcap isn't in a direct relationship with the trees, it is playing a key part in the relationship between the trees and a parasite that can cause them damage.[98] It is a great example of how interrelated the world of nature is, and how a change in behaviour (our feeding of birds in the winter) can lead to completely unforeseen changes in other species. You might not have thought that putting out peanuts and fat balls would lead to an increase in the parasitic load that some of our trees endure – but that appears to be exactly what is happening.

The bird–berry relationship is probably one of the best known and most widely documented examples of mutualistic symbiotic relationships that exist between the trees and the birds. Not all seeds, though, are wrapped in berries; some are hidden within more woody structures, but this doesn't preclude them from being dispersed by birds. So let's have a look at two different seed casings produced by two very different types of tree, which nevertheless share a common denominator when it comes to the dispersal of their seeds. That common denominator is corvids, members of the crow family with prodigious memories. Those different trees use different birds from this family to carry out a similar task; sadly, though, for the first of these relationships the future is not looking bright.

Changing climates

The whitebark pine is a beautiful tree found high up on the mountain ranges of eastern North America, straddling the border of Canada and the United States. It is usually the last tree to be found in these ranges before altitude exacts its power, the whitebarks forming the treeline, the edge of existence as far as trees are concerned. Because of where the whitebark pine grows, it can form trees that are known as krummholz,[99] trees that are so buckled and

---

98 We tend to look at mistletoe as a benign thing, a pretty adornment on the bare winter branches, but it is a parasite that takes much-needed water and nutrients from trees. A single mistletoe plant may have minimal effect on the tree, but infestations of it can lead to reduced growth and even loss of large branches. Very heavy infestations may weaken the tree sufficiently to cause its death.

99 From the German for 'crooked wood'.

deformed by their harsh growing conditions that they are often no more than stunted ground-hugging examples.

However, below the treeline and away from exposure to its fierce, bitingly cold, winds the whitebark pine is more typical in form, growing to 30 metres in height. It has the usual pine tree foliage – long green needles held in bunches of five[100] – and it has pine cones. Although these structures can be very varied across the conifer spectrum of species, those of pine trees generally conform to our idea of what a cone should look like.

The cones of the whitebark pine do exactly that; they are small woody structures of around 7 cm in length. Cones protect and house the developing seeds inside, and sometimes these cones can take years to ripen. If we look at the familiar Scots pine, we find its cones take two years to mature, then, in warm sunny spring weather the cone's woody scales crack open, releasing the small seeds to be borne by the wind to potential germination sites. The vast majority of cones produced by pines need heat as the mechanism to open them, be that from sunlight or the more extreme heat of forest fires. But the cones of the whitebark pine don't use heat to release their seeds. They use a completely different method – it's a bird, a beautiful bird, the Clark's nutcracker.

Clark's nutcracker is a member of the crow family and is actually closely related to Europe's species of nutcracker, the spotted nutcracker, although plumagewise the two are very different. Clark's nutcracker is a beautiful soft dove-grey bird with a piercing pair of black eyes and an equally black bill; its wings and tail are black, flashed with white markings. It is an easily recognised and very attractive avian dinosaur indeed.

They live in high mountain forests, taking in the range of the whitebark pine on whose seeds they feed – but they don't feed on these seeds alone; they are typical corvids in that they are omnivorous and are always ready to take advantage of new feeding opportunities. In recent years they have even taken to walking into campers' tents to scavenge (or steal) the food supplies within! But the camper bonanza is only available in the summer months. During the winter, times are much harder and food can be scarce, but the Clark's nutcracker has planned ahead for this lean time, laying down a supply of food to see it through.

Its food of choice for these winter larders is pine seed; principally those of the whitebark pine and the closely related limber pine, but also the seeds of other pine species. While the bird eats and stores a lot of whitebark pine seeds, it doesn't specialise in them.

However, the whitebark pine *does* specialise in the Clark's nutcracker; the bird is the tree's sole seed disperser. It is a long-evolved relationship; when the cones are ripe they have to be prised open to expose the seeds inside, and the nutcracker's bill is the ideal tool for that.

These seeds make excellent food for a bird that has to cope with extreme alpine conditions; they are made up of around 21 per cent protein and 51 per cent fat, and the birds feed on them greedily. But in eating the seeds, digesting their protein-rich and fatty contents, they

---

100 Pine trees generally produce needles in bunches of two, three or five needles. There is an exception, the single-leaf pinyon, the only one of around 111 pine species to have singular needles.

destroy them. If a whitebark pine seed has been eaten by a Clark's nutcracker, it doesn't pass through the gut unharmed; it is digested. So it won't germinate.

Why, then, has the tree evolved a relationship with the bird?

It comes down to storage; the nutcracker stores prodigious amounts of the whitebark's seeds; one study estimated that a single bird can store up to an incredible 98,000 of them in the autumnal fruiting season! Whitebark pines produce an abundance of seed-producing cones every two to three years, but they don't do so universally; while one area may have trees producing a plethora of cones, other areas won't, so the distribution of the bonanza is patchy. This means that birds that wish to exploit it have to travel to do so. Areas of whitebark pines that are producing lots of seed-bearing cones attract large numbers of Clark's nutcrackers, the birds flying in from all around to gather and then cache the seeds. Birds have been recorded flying over 20 miles to collect the seeds, then back to their territories to store them, sometimes making ten such journeys a day. That's over 400 miles' flying. The Clark's nutcracker certainly seems aware of how important this food source is to it.

The nutcracker caches these seeds in small groups by burying them in the ground. This avian act of burial is also an arboreal act of planting, the birds depositing the tree's seed in the soil, the very place where the seed needs to be if it's going to germinate. The bird then relies on its memory to find these cached seeds again once winter has arrived. It is very, very good at remembering where it has cached them; studies have shown that they can remember their locations for up to nine months. This amazing memory must surely be a bad thing for the tree – after all, the seeds won't germinate if they are found and eaten. But the Clark's nutcracker isn't just a bird with a great memory, it is also a bird that likes to err on the side of caution, and it is estimated that a single bird will cache around twice as much seed as it is going to need. This over-caching is an insurance policy on the part of the bird, putting away (quite) a bit extra, just in case. The whitebark pine relies on the fact that most insurance policies are never cashed in.

Now it should be said that the Clark's nutcracker is a rather inefficient partner for the tree, as it doesn't always cache the seeds in appropriate places for them to germinate, preferring to select sites that are under cover of dense branches, to keep them accessible in times of heavy snowfall. But for the tree's seeds to be successful they require lots of sunlight and exposure to colder temperatures; the ideal sites from the tree's perspective are those that are likely to get covered in heavy snow. It has been estimated that only around 16 per cent of the seeds collected by the Clark's nutcracker will be deposited in caches that will actually assist their germination.

That sounds low – a poor return for the tree having evolved a relationship with the bird – but looking at the numbers rather than the percentage gives a different picture. It has been estimated that a single whitebark pine tree will produce over a million seeds in its lifetime. As 16 per cent of a million is 160,000, that's a lot of seeds placed in suitable germination spots. Suddenly the statistic looks rather healthy.

So, high up in the North American continent, often a long way from humans, this relationship has evolved into a mutualistically beneficial one. The tree has developed cones that need to be opened by the bird. The bird does this using its bill that serves the purpose perfectly, it then takes the seed from the cone, and whilst the vast majority of these get eaten, a still significant number of them have the chance to germinate. The bird gets a great food to help it survive the winter months, and the tree gets its seeds dispersed. What could go wrong?

The usual: us. The balanced relationship between the bird and the tree has been greatly upset in recent years, so much so that the whitebark pine is in serious danger of extinction. The IUCN is now listing it as an endangered species. What have we done to cause this? Have we introduced another species into their midst? Have we over-exploited the timber of the tree? Have we hunted the bird to near-extinction? Have we destroyed the habitat through insensitive land use?

It is none of these; the reason is much more insidious and much more difficult to rectify, let alone stop. We have changed the climate.

Climate change is a massive threat to so many species on this planet. Our actions in releasing vast amount of carbon dioxide and other gases into the atmosphere even threatens our own existence. Global heating is already leading to changing weather patterns and rising sea levels. You don't need me to tell you that human-induced climate change is a really bad thing. For species that live in the extreme conditions of high mountain ranges it poses a particular challenge; as the climate warms, the cold mountain conditions that some species require are literally moved upwards – but when you're already living on the top of a mountain there's nowhere else to go.

We are seeing this in our own country; the dwarf birch, a species I mentioned at the beginning of this book, is now in serious threat of extinction in Britain as its mountainous niche is forced ever upwards. A fantastic bird, the ptarmigan, is also being forced higher and higher. But mountains are not infinite, and it too is in trouble in Britain as a result of the changing climate.

In the case of the whitebark pine, though, the tree is not being forced higher by the increasing warmth of the changing climate; it is instead being attacked on two fronts, first by a fungus and secondly by an insect, attacks that are caused by the changing climate. Except the word 'attacked' doesn't quite cover it; the tree is being decimated by the double whammy that climate change has brought with it. The fungus is the white pine blister rust, and it's endemic to Europe. There it has coevolved with white pine species such as the stone pine so there's a balance in place. But the white pines of America (of which the whitebark is one) didn't coevolve with the fungus and have no such protection, and as a result are very vulnerable to it. The fungal pathogen was introduced to North America in 1900 and although there were outbreaks, its activities and impact were relatively limited – until recently.

But the warming climate has changed that; the pathogen can now survive in areas where before it couldn't, areas that bring it into the domain of the high-altitude whitebark pine.

The fungus is a slow attacker, but a persistent one, causing necrosis in the branches it affects, killing the tree over a period of a few years.

The fungus would be bad enough, but combined with a small insignificant-looking beetle, the overall impact on the whitebark pine has been catastrophic. The mountain pine beetle is a native species of bark beetle found in the mountains of western North America, and as its name suggests, it lives out its life cycle in a variety of pine species that grow in mountain ranges. It lays its eggs under the bark, and the larvae feed on the phloem layer, the vital part of a living tree. Like the elm bark beetle, it can introduce fungal pathogens into the tree. It has always been a natural part of life in these high montane forests, a part of the ecosystem, kept in check by harsh winters. Its larvae have always fed on the trees but it has generally only had a terminal effect on older and unhealthy ones.

But climate change has altered the playing field drastically. Since the year 2000, the climate has warmed enough for the beetle to breed in higher altitudes, where it was unable to do so before. That means it can now complete its breeding cycle in whitebark pine in one year, reproducing again and again without the winter killing it off. As a result, the mountain pine beetle's population has grown exponentially, and so has the damage it wreaks. All white pine trees are now vulnerable to it, and they are being killed by it: not just the old and sick ones, but young healthy ones, and not in their ones or twos but in their thousands. Whole hillsides have turned from being blanketed in vibrant green needles to areas of stark grey trunks.

The combination of the beetle and fungus has proved too much for many parts of this ecosystem. In Yellowstone National Park it has been reported that 750,000 whitebark pines have been killed – that's over 35 per cent of the whitebarks there – and it is believed that another 38 per cent are about to join them. In some parts of Alberta in Canada there are areas with 100 per cent die-off. Since the year 2000 around 48 million acres of Canadian forest have been, as one report put it, massacred. In the United States it is estimated that 41 million acres of pine forest are either dead or dying.

This obviously has severe implications for the unique montane forest ecosystems of these areas. The ecology of these forests, like all forests, is interconnected, and the whitebark pine plays a key role in retaining soil and slowing meltwater runoff, in turn providing habitat for tiny plants – and food for massive mammals; the seeds of the pine aren't eaten by Clark's nutcracker alone but are also an important fatty food source for grizzly bears before they enter hibernation.[101]

What the implications will be for the other species in the whitebark pine habitats isn't clear at the moment, but it isn't going to be good.

The Clark's nutcracker – the other half of the symbiotic relationship between tree and bird – seems to be holding its own, as it has the advantage of being omnivorous, including

---

101 The bears raid the middens of squirrels that also feed on the cones, stashing them in small piles on the ground which the bear, using its prodigious sense of smell, can easily find even beneath the snow.

eating other tree seeds, seeds which it can store in much the same way it stores the seeds of the whitebark. The bird can switch food sources. They can also move.

But the trees can't do that. They are where they are, and even if they somehow survive the onslaught of the fungus and the beetle, they may then find themselves without their number one seed disperser.

Because although the population of the nutcracker is not falling, it's shifting. There have been steep localised declines in the bird's numbers in areas where the whitebark once grew in abundance. This isn't surprising; why would the bird stay in a dead forest? The worry is, though, that as the birds abandon these areas they may also lose the connection they had with them. Young Clark's nutcrackers follow their parents to feed when the trees produce their cones, but if the cones aren't there the adults don't go, and if they don't go, the young don't learn the location. The chain is broken.

It is likely that in the whitebark population there will be a percentage – probably a very small percentage – of trees that are resistant or partially resistant to the depredations of both the fungus and the beetle. If they can produce seeds, then those seeds will also be resistant, and slowly, very slowly, this resistance can subsequently build up in the tree population. But it can only do so if the Clark's nutcracker is present to disperse the seeds. If the bird has abandoned the forest because the vast majority of its trees have died, the very few trees that survive are already functionally dead.[102] Things are looking very bleak for the whitebark pine and its symbiotic relationship with the Clark's nutcracker.

What is happening in the high mountain forests of North America is more than likely being repeated across the globe. Climate change poses an existentialist threat to a myriad species and to the long-evolved relationships they have with other species. The vast majority of these relationships will be ones that we don't even know about, but our ignorance of their existence doesn't stop them from being under threat.

The second relationship that involves a corvid, its memory and a seed encased in a woody structure is a relationship that is currently much healthier – and, in contrast to that between the whitebark pine and the Clark's nutcracker, it is one that has helped the tree enormously in a warming climate.

If you ask a British person to name a tree, the odds are that they will say 'oak'. This is a family of trees that don't produce their seeds within tasty berries, or woody cones, but like the unrelated cone-bearing conifers their seeds are encased in a woody structure, a structure we have named an acorn. It is time to turn our attention back to the beginning of this book, to revisit that magnificent pedunculate oak growing in the middle of a field.

---

102 A species is said to be functionally extinct if it has lost the means to reproduce; for example, the last-ever passenger pigeon survived alone in a zoo for a number of years, but during that time, with no mate to breed with and even though she was very much still alive, the passenger pigeon was functionally extinct. I have just adapted the phrase to fit.

From small acorns grow …

The English oak is a name that has become a bit of a cliché; it is a somewhat jingoistic label that is used to describe one of two species native to Britain within the very large oak genus.[103] These two species are the sessile oak and the pedunculate oak. Of these two, it is the latter that is normally referred to as the English oak, despite the fact that it is equally native to Scotland, Wales and Ireland. So it is a poor moniker for a United Kingdom tree – but it is even poorer when you consider this iconic tree's natural range. Growing from the Atlantic coast of Portugal in the west to the shores of the Caspian Sea in the east, and from the toe of Italy in the south to Norway in the north, this is a very widespread European tree indeed. Its extent in England is in reality a very small part of its true native range.[104] But the name has stuck, and for many English people any oak tree that they see, whether a pedunculate or a sessile,[105] is simply an English oak.

For a tree, or any other species for that matter, to be considered native to Britain, it has to have arrived here without the help of us humans, before the rising sea levels after the last ice age flooded the lowlands of what are now the southern end of the North Sea and the eastern end of the Channel. From that point onwards, as the waves lapped over the land, Britain became an island, cut off from the rest of the continental land mass. The salt-laden sea water has proved to be an insurmountable barrier for most living species, especially trees.

Not all of what would become the British Isles was under permanent ice during the last ice age, but those parts not under ice were still very cold; the ice-free landscape was one of tundra. It was not a place for trees. As the permanent ice cap retreated and the tundra warmed it also began to change, and the landscape of low, slow-growing plants became available for other, bigger, faster growing plants to colonise.

As the temperature rose, the tree species that would become our natives spread northwards from their temperature-enforced exile in the south of Europe. Some trees were able to spread rapidly; pioneer species like the birches can produce prodigious amounts of seed, and these tiny, wind-borne packages of potential can be blown far and wide.

---

103 Worldwide, the oak genus *Quercus* has around 500 species within it. These are spread right around the northern hemisphere, the greatest diversity found in Mexico, a country that has 160 native species of oak. The majority of oak species are evergreen and do not shed their leaves like our two species.

104 Geographical data taken from the internet resource Chorological Maps for the Main European Woody Species, Caudullo, G. et al.

105 The two species are very similar; the best way of telling them apart is the acorns. Those of the sessile, as the name suggests, lack a stalk and are borne in a cup growing directly off the twig. The pedunculate's acorns are also borne in cups, but these cups have thin stalks connecting them to the twigs, giving them an almost Popeye pipe appearance.

Our two widespread native species of birch – yes, there are two of these as well[106] – were among the first of those pioneers, along with the likes of the goat willow, to colonise the land that would later become the British Isles.

Other species followed them, taking advantage of the geological window of almost 2,000 years that lay between the initial retreat of the ice sheets and the flooding of the land that linked us to mainland Europe around 8,500 years ago. Two millennia may sound like a long time to us humans, but in reality it was only a short window of opportunity for the trees. Once those salty waters had risen, it was no longer possible for trees to naturally colonise Britain. Over 40[107] species of tree, though, did make it through that metaphoric window before the rising sea levels slammed it shut, isolating Britain from the rest of Europe. Many of the trees that did so are rapid colonisers, as you would expect – trees that are perfectly adapted to take advantage of the opportunity presented by the retreating ice sheets and tundra. But some are not as well adapted to such rapid colonisation; the common beech, a truly majestic tree familiar to us all, almost didn't make it to Britain. Indeed, there are some biologists that believe it didn't actually get here before the land bridge went, and that it was latterly introduced by us humans; however those biologists are definitely in a minority, the vast majority believing that the beech did make it here by its own means – though only just, the tree considered to be native only to the very south-east of England.

As we know, however, the two oaks, the pedunculate and the sessile, did get here in time; in fact they got here in relatively quick time, even managing to outpace trees like the common ash and the small-leaved lime – trees whose seeds are light and winged and carried by the wind, trees that on paper should have got here long before the oaks ever did. But we know from extensive pollen records that the ash and the limes didn't colonise the land that would become Britain until after the two oaks had. That raises the question: how did the oaks do that? How did they manage to advance northwards so quickly?

Oak seeds, the familiar acorns, are not exactly highly mobile – they are far too heavy to be dispersed by the wind, and they have no wings[108] to exploit air currents. Indeed, when they are ripe they drop straight down from the tree; although they might bounce a bit, they certainly wouldn't have been able to bounce far enough for the trees to get to Britain within that relatively short geological window.

---

106 These are the silver birch and the equally common downy birch. Many people, including many naturalists, seem blind to the fact that the downy birch exists, referring to any birch they see as a silver birch.

107 There are roughly 77 species of tree that are considered to be native to the British Isles, but a large number of these are members of the *Sorbus* genus, the whitebeams, and these are species that evolved after the land bridge disappeared beneath the waves, these Whitebeam species are unique to Britain, we have species of trees that are found nowhere else on Earth.

108 Technically known as samaras, flattened areas of papery tissue emanating from the seed case that catch the wind as they fall. Ash keys and maple helicopters are the classic examples.

No, for the oaks to spread north so rapidly, to make it here before the land bridge went, before that window was closed, they needed to have help, avian help.

The jay is a truly beautiful bird, a lovely mix of pinkish grey, splashed with black and white, with a fantastic flash of electric blue on the wings. It is an exotic-looking member of the crow family and is widespread across Britain, but unlike its blacker relatives, the jay tends to be shy, preferring the depths of woodland, especially oak woodland, to more open habitats. Jays, like the aforementioned Clark's nutcracker and most other members of the corvid family, have a very varied diet, eating a wide range of invertebrates, seeds and fruit, and in the spring young birds and eggs.[109] But what the jay really loves to eat is the acorn.

Jay

---

109 Dietary data taken from the excellent book *Crows and Jays* by Steve Madge and Hilary Burn. Christopher Helm, 1994.

In the autumn months jays are prodigious feeders on acorns; they will travel far and wide to find trees that are fruiting, leaving their normally strictly regulated territories to do so. But the seasonal abundance of acorns only lasts for a short period of time, and the jay really likes eating them, so to make sure that it can go on enjoying these large and nutritious seeds long after the season has finished, it stores them so that it can return to them and feed on the oak's bounty throughout the winter and even well into the next spring. This is a bird that thinks ahead and stocks up. It is a strategy that mirrors exactly the strategy of its North American cousin.

Like many of the corvid family, jays are considered to be intelligent birds, and there have been many studies of this intelligence; a group of jays at Cambridge University have even learnt to use human speech in their interactions with researchers! If you have a few minutes to spare, search on the internet for the video of talking jays at Cambridge University; it is rather brilliant.[110] Apart from talking our language, or at least mimicking it, one aspect considered to be a sign of intelligence in animals is the ability to deliberately cache food in a planned and methodical way. We have already seen that corvids can do this with other tree species, and when it comes to oaks and methodically caching their acorns, the jay is an absolute master.

It doesn't cache just a few acorns to consume at a later date – it caches lots and lots of them. One research study in Germany recorded 65 colour-ringed jays over a period of four weeks during the autumn acorn season. Between them in just those 28 days, the birds cached half a million acorns: that's almost 7,700 acorns each! So on average each jay in the study cached around 275 acorns every single day. Another piece of research on this bird's caching behaviour has concluded that in Britain jays cache around one and a half *billion* acorns each year. This incredible, but entirely credible, number doesn't include the acorns that the jays eat there and then when foraging, but are just the ones the birds fly off with to cache for later consumption. If you have ever wondered where the acorns that adorned the oaks near you disappear to each year, the jay is most probably the answer! The beautiful jay is, without any doubt, the acorn bird, a fact that is reflected in its scientific name of *Garrulus glandarius*, 'chattering [bird] of acorns'.

It might be thought that the jay's gluttonous appetite for acorns would be disadvantageous to the oaks, but of course the opposite is true. It can easily be deduced by the amount of time that these corvids expend on their feeding and caching of acorns that the two oak species are key trees for the bird, but it also can be said that the jay is a key species for the oaks. Quite simply, the jay is the main propagator of the oaks of Britain and Europe, and has been long before we humans started planting trees.[111] It is yet another example of a mutualistic symbiotic relationship between the trees and the birds. Jays are birds with astonishing

---

110 Jays haven't learnt our language; instead, they are superb mimics, and there have been many times when their expert mimicry of other bird's calls has totally fooled me.

111 *Forest and Woodland Trees in Britain*, John White. Oxford University Press 1995.

memories – memories that enable them to locate acorns they have cached many months before – but even these memorious birds will forget some of the many thousands they have hidden. And, of course, when a jay gets predated – by a goshawk[112] for example – it is not just the bird that dies, but also the locations of the thousands of acorns it has cached. It is from these small acorns that mighty oaks do grow.

Oak trees produce a heavy shade; they can have around a quarter of a million sunlight-hungry leaves in their canopies.[113] These leaves absorb a lot of light and cast a lot of shade, but this shade makes it difficult for the tree's own seedlings, if on the ground beneath their parent tree, to germinate successfully. A problem that has been exacerbated in the last 120 years or so by what the late (and very great) tree historian Oliver Rackham termed 'oak change'.[114] In a mast year[115] an oak of either of our two native species can produce around 10,000 individual acorns, a visit to an oak woodland on a windy autumnal day can be quite exciting as these hard seeds thud into the leaf litter. This can result in up to 100 of them per square metre littering the floor underneath a parent tree. This amount of seed concentrated in such a tiny shady space constitutes a waste of the tree's precious resources – after all, the tree, like any other living organism, is simply trying to produce as much progeny as it possibly can. What the oaks need for these valuable seeds is a distributor – and the jay, as the numbers show, is the acorn distributor par excellence.

Jays have what could be described as a throat pocket, a 'gular pouch', an enlarged area in its throat. Whether you call it a pocket or a pouch, it is perfect, and no doubt evolved to be so, for storing acorns. Jays can easily fit four acorns into this handy space as well as carrying another one in its bill, allowing the bird to take at least five at a time, but some birds have even been observed to carry nine![116] Once loaded up with these acorns, the jay proceeds to cache them, but it doesn't cache them close to the tree – it takes them away; usually around 50–60 metres, but sometimes much, much further. Some birds fly several kilometres[117] before they carefully hide their arboreal treasure.

It is at this point that the oak tree starts to potentially benefit from its relationship with

---

112 When I used to monitor pairs of goshawk under licence in British forests, I would often find the distinctive feathers of the jay on the plucking posts of these powerful raptors.

113 Leaf numbers taken from the book, *The Long, Long Life of Trees*, Fiona Stafford. Yale University Press 2016.

114 Oliver Rackham wrote some fantastic books; *The History of the British Countryside* and *Trees and Woodlands in the British Landscape* are absolute classics and must-reads. He used the term 'oak change' to denote how our native oak species have seemingly stopped regenerating within our woodlands.

115 A year in which a tree produces a bumper seed crop.

116 Nine acorn data taken from RSPB web site.

117 One bird has even been recorded carrying an acorn for 20 kilometres before it cached it.

the jay. Once it has chosen its site, the corvid caches its collection of acorns by using its bill to force the individual acorns into the ground, carefully hammering them into the soil. This sounds like rough handling, but jays are gentle couriers, taking care to not damage the acorns when it gathers them, transports them, and caches them. Finally, once it has put the undamaged seed into the ground, it covers it over with leaf litter, soil, grass or other substrate. In other words, it plants it.

This could well be a deliberate tactic on behalf of the bird, for jays are known to use the germinating oak saplings in the late spring as a clue to finding the nutritious bounty they had cached maybe eight months before. After such an extended period of time has passed, it is likely that whilst the jay can remember the rough site where it cached the acorn, it is unlikely to remember the precise location – but a seedling poking up through the ground indicates to the bird exactly where the food was buried. 'Planting' acorns definitely helps the jay find them again many months later, but it also helps the oaks.

Jays may hoard acorns, but when it comes to caching them they do so singularly; they don't put all of their proverbial eggs in one basket. This reduces the chances of their larder being destroyed by other animals such as foraging wild boar.[118] If a boar was to find a whole stash of acorns it would devour them, emptying the bird's food resources at one stroke, but if the boar is only able to find individual acorns, the effect this discovery will have on the bird's stored food source is minimal. Numerous studies have shown that the buried acorns are often spaced around a metre apart, a pattern very similar to our own when we plant trees. Any acorns that are forgotten, or lost due to the death of the planter, find themselves in the perfect position to germinate and grow rapidly.

But if the planter returns to the newly germinated oak, it is not necessarily a disaster for the young tree. Whilst it certainly doesn't look great for the fledgling oak, the actual impact on the young tree is surprisingly minimal. Before the oak appears above the ground it has germinated below it, rapidly developing a strong network of nourishment-providing roots. These roots negate the need for the young seedling to rely on the food resources stored in the acorn; it is the roots, not the acorn, that provide the majority of the biological fuel required for the tree to sprout and develop its first true leaves. If you are lucky enough to see a jay pulling up a young oak, you will notice that it lifts it only just enough to get the acorn and the energy contained within it; the bird doesn't actually uproot the tree. It just gives the acorn a smart tug and a quick snip, and off it goes, leaving the still-rooted seedling to continue growing. It is tempting to think that the acorn is nothing more than a final payment from the young tree to the jay for its successful planting.

If you find an oak tree growing in the open countryside, or germinating in your lawn,

---

118 Jays take the threat of their cache being discovered by others very seriously. One study published by the Royal Society in 2013 showed that jays, when another jay or potential competitor is nearby, will select a site that has a relatively quiet substrate in which to bury their acorns. The study concluded that the bird is selecting that site to avoid making noises that could be interpreted by the other bird as a sign that food is being stored.

or – as I often do – appearing in your veg patch,[119] it is highly likely that it was planted by this feathered forester. Jays avoid caching (or planting) the acorns under mature trees where possible, positively selecting non-shaded habitats instead; this can be a large woodland glade, but often it is away from woodland altogether, alongside field edges and within grassland. Why the jay does this is not known, but it does raise some intriguing questions; does the jay know that the oaks don't germinate so readily in shady conditions? Is the bird deliberately caching the acorn in a spot that will be propitious to the seed sprouting in the spring, making it easier for the bird to retrieve it?

It would be easy to think that – but to do so would discount the fact that the birds return to the majority of their cached acorns to feed on them long before the seeds germinate. Perhaps the jay chooses these sites because in a more open landscape it is able to better orientate itself and therefore is more easily able to recognise landmarks that will help it recall the location when it comes looking for the acorns at a later date. Whatever the reason for the bird's caching behaviour, one thing is for certain; the jay is distributing the acorns over a far wider area than the tree itself could ever do. There are mammals that cache acorns, but they often damage them in the process, whereas the jays' much more meticulous handling means that the seeds stay viable. The other major difference between acorn caching in mammals and in birds is that the bird can distribute the acorns over a far wider area than can any land-bound mammal.

Let's go back to the end of the last glaciation period of the most recent Ice Age, a time when the world is warming up. The tundra that has covered so much of the continent is rapidly thawing, exposing immense areas of potential for bigger plants, and the oak trees in the forest refuges of southern Europe are producing acorns in abundance. The jays are loading their gular pouches with acorns before taking to the wing to seek open ground in which to cache them. And where is this open ground? It is to the north and it is vast – every spring sees thousands of oak saplings germinating north of their parent oaks. This happens year after year, decade after decade – new oak trees springing forth, expanding the tree's range towards the north and what will become Britain.

Both the pedunculate and the sessile oak made it long before the rising sea levels cut Britain off from the continent, but they couldn't have done it without the jay. Without this beautiful woodland bird embarking on its annual acorn-planting bonanza, the oaks would not have been able to spread northwards.[120] Without this amazing relationship between the bird and the tree, the pedunculate oak and the sessile oak would not be native to Britain, and the concept of the English oak would not exist.

Take a minute to think what this would mean. The name 'English oak' came about

---

119 What with the jays and blackbirds, my veg patch is always on the verge of becoming a mini tree nursery!

120 There have been many scientific papers published on this subject, the paper published in 1982 by Henry Howe and Judith Smallwood entitled 'Ecology of Seed Dispersal' the one most often quoted.

because these trees have played a fundamental part in the culture and history of the country of England. The symbolism of the oak can be found everywhere in our everyday lives, its leaves and acorns often used as logos, proudly displaying membership of organisations or as a symbol of a 'natural' or 'English' product that we should be proud to buy. It was the timber of our oaks that fuelled our shipbuilding and the resulting expansion of our nation's horizons and ambitions, Sir Francis Drake, Sir Walter Raleigh, Captain Cook – they all sailed in ships hewn from the native oaks of our woodlands.

The oak even became a metaphor for the characteristics of the Englishman, the Georgian poet William Shenstone in particular making reference to the perceived shared qualities of the English male and the steadfast tree, qualities of strength, reliability and composure. And in doing this he ignored our fellow countries within the British Isles, and women everywhere. Prior to this, John Evelyn in his monumental 1664 work *Sylva* made substantial reference to the oak and its vital importance to the nation, in particular to the navy and the importance that it bestowed on us as a country. HMS *Victory*,[121] arguably our most famous battleship, is a good example of how important oak was to the British navy. It was made using the timber of around 6,000 trees, 90 per cent of them oak. This is roughly the equivalent of 100 acres of mature woodland.[122] Let's not forget that *Victory* was just one of 27 British ships in action at the Battle of Trafalgar. That's an enormous number of oaks. The British colonies, and later its empire, were all built on our ability as seafarers, and our seafaring nature was built of oak. Without oak, the history of Britain would have been very different indeed – and it is that history, both the good and the bad, that shapes our nation today. What we are, who we are, all comes from a corvid's predilection for acorns.

That might seem a trifle hyperbolic, but it is something I believe to be true. It is, of course, equally true to say that if the oaks hadn't made it to what is now Britain before the sea levels rose, one or both of those two native species would certainly have been introduced at a later date – after all, we are now home to far more species of introduced trees than we are to native ones. But the vast majority of the introduced species weren't introduced until after we had started sailing the world's seas; in other words we didn't start introducing tree species until after we had become masters of using our home-grown oak timbers to build ships. Britain today is down to the jays. If Britain ever requires a national bird, there can surely only be one contender.[123]

Even if oaks had been introduced by the Romans – and they would have been a likely source, having introduced the sweet chestnut during their time in Britain – it is highly

---

121 Nelson's famous flagship was actually launched in 1765 – that's 40 years before Trafalgar, the battle in which it became a legend. On its launch Lord Nelson himself was only seven years of age.

122 Data taken from the HMS *Victory* website.

123 In 2015 the birdwatcher David Lindo launched a poll to declare which bird should be the unofficial official bird of Britain. Over 200,000 people voted, and the winner was the robin; sadly, the jay didn't even register.

The Mighty Oak

unlikely that they would have done so on a scale sufficiently large enough to create the vast areas of natural oak woodland that we so heavily exploited just a millennium or so later. John Evelyn's work was, above all else, a plea to replenish our woodlands; he recognised that we were running out of oaks (and other species), and that the supply of usable timber generated by these trees was running low. This plea came about despite the fact that oaks had been spreading and growing in Britain for over 8,000 years. If they had been introduced at a later date there just wouldn't have been enough of them available to be exploited on the vast scale that they were.

Last autumn I watched a jay gathering acorns from underneath a pedunculate oak on the slopes of northern Dartmoor. The bird was hopping busily about the ground, picking up the fallen fruits of the tree, assessing their viability as a foodstuff, occasionally dismissing one that didn't make the grade. Those that did were quickly swallowed into its internal pocket. As I watched its colours gleaming in the autumn sunshine, I couldn't help wondering whether the tree it was gathering acorns from was a tree that a jay, many decades before, had planted as it too cached its own acorns carefully, perhaps also on a sunny day. The jay I was watching finished collecting up what it could hold of the tree's bounty, and with its throat bulging, the normally wary bird then flew right over me, heading towards open land to plant its acorns. I watched its white rump disappear into the distance and continued my wondering. Perhaps, in generations to come, someone else will watch a jay gathering acorns under a tree that germinated from this very bird's load. Maybe they too will reflect on the relationship between the oaks and the jay, a relationship that has had very profound consequences for us on these islands we call home.

Epilogue

I am back in the verdant field once more, standing by the large pedunculate oak, beneath its sprawling branches. I place my hand on the tree's corpulent trunk, feeling the rigid strength of it. My eyes trace the innumerable pathways created by the ridges and crevices in this venerable tree's bark; I follow them downwards to the soil and visualise the network of roots that must spread below me just as the canopy spreads itself above. I wonder to myself if, all those years ago in its first spring of life, a colourful member of the corvid family hopped across to it, clasped it in its bill and pulled it up slightly before taking the acorn from which it had grown.

My eyes retrace their route back up the large stem and continue following the pathways upward, past the first of the large branches, before it becomes impossible for me to continue my visual meandering up the interconnected criss-cross pattern of channels. The leaves of the tree are still a fresh green, yet to darken and harden off, still lacking the bitter tannins that will help protect them. They are vulnerable right now, vulnerable to a large army of invertebrates that are probably already munching on the leaves above me. I wonder, as I look, whether the tree is releasing its chemical signals in response to the assault, signals undetectable by me, but detectable by other oaks and quite probably birds.

The connections and relationships that this tree has, and has had, with the other species of this field, be they avian dinosaurs or microscopic fungi, are probably as involved and numerous as the pathways along its bark that I have been attempting to follow. My eyes struggle to follow these interconnected bark-bound routes, and if I can't easily follow these visible pathways …

There is so much we don't see when we look at the natural world, so much we don't understand. There are ecological relationships all around us. Those between the trees and the birds are relatively easy to spot, but we still don't know about all of them, and those we do know about aren't necessarily fully understood.

As I turn to go, a movement in the branches above catches my attention. A blue tit is flitting around their very tips, grabbing the thin twigs with its even thinner legs, enabling it to hang acrobatically as it gleans the newly emerged leaves for caterpillars. I watch it work, watch its diligence as it scours the leaves, carefully adding the larvae it finds to the others in its bill. Then it drops its grip, opens its wings and flies across the canopy to one of the large branches that radiate out from trunk on the other side of the tree. It lands beside a hole, the remnant socket of a discarded branch. It looks about, looks at me, and disappears inside.

As I walk through the grass, heading back down to the farm buildings by the lane, I hear the harsh screeching raucous cry of a jay emanating from somewhere far off. As I open the gate a broad smile breaks across my face.

Acknowledgements

There are many people that I need to thank, not least Keith Whittles and Sue Stevens at Whittles Publishing, both of whom have been supportive of my writings. This is my third book with them, but without their enthusiasm for my first book it is unlikely that this one would have ever been written. So thank you to them and their team.

I would like to thank Gerard Gorman, who was happy and ready to share his knowledge of woodpeckers with me, despite having never met me. Thank you, Gerard, much appreciated. Thanks also to Stuart Gillies for kindly allowing the use of his photo of a great spotted woodpecker.

I would also like to thank Kenton Rogers of Treeconomics, who, despite me surfacing out of the blue after many a year had passed, was more than happy to discuss with me the ins and outs of tree hole development.

There have been many authors that have written great books either on or featuring trees that I have enjoyed over the years. I would like to thank two of them specifically, even though, sadly, my thanks are posthumous. Alan Mitchell was the Forestry Commission's dendrologist from 1970 onwards, and by all accounts his knowledge of trees was unsurpassable. In 1972 he wrote the Forestry Commission Booklet 33 'Conifers in the British Isles, a descriptive handbook', a monumental work which has often helped me over the years to identify tricky examples of this large group. But his greatest work, in my opinion, was published in 1996. It was entitled *Alan Mitchell's Trees of Britain*. Alan had a passion for recording trees, their growth rates and their vital statistics, and that book is a culmination of his passion; it lists the biggest, oldest, tallest and finest of the trees that grow in Britain. That might make it sound like a book of statistics, but it is so much more than that. This book inspired me to start looking at trees more closely, to be awed by them. Alan died in 1995, just as my own career with the Forestry Commission as a ranger was developing, so I never got to meet him. I wish I had.

The second author I would like to record my thanks to is Roger Deakin, a superb writer with a fantastically engaging style. His book *Wildwood, a Journey through Trees* is the best natural history book I have ever read. It is beautiful. Again, Roger is someone who I never met, someone who I wished I could have shared time with, walking through trees. When Roger died in 2006, he left a legacy to help other authors, a legacy that is administered by the Society of Authors through their Authors' Foundation grant scheme. I am proud to say that I was awarded a grant from this legacy to help me write this book, and I am extremely grateful. Thank you.

I would like to thank Matt Merritt, the editor of *Bird Watching* magazine for kindly publishing my articles and for being supportive to my writing. I'd also like to thank Mark Avery, for being an inspirational conservationist and for allowing me to publish blogs on his website. Seeing my writings in the magazine and on the website have been tremendous boosts to my confidence, especially when I was beginning as a writer.

Writing a book takes a tremendous amount of time, and whilst you are writing the book you are not earning any money from it. I would therefore like to thank Gary Cleverdon for giving me the opportunity to earn some money as well as for giving me the time off required to write. There aren't many who would do so. Thank you.

Finally, I would like to thank Kate for the inspiration. And to thank Jo for absolutely everything.

Appendix 1 – Species mentioned in the text

The way we name species can be very confusing, especially when it comes to listing the species I have mentioned in this book. Species can have more than one common name, or name it's known by, which can be a shortened version of its 'official' common name. To try and avoid confusion and complication, I have chosen to list each species by its common name, as generally shown in the popular field guides.

In some cases I have added frequently used epithets for a species when it is necessary to distinguish it from other closely related species, but otherwise I have omitted those epithets. Thus I have listed the common hawthorn to distinguish it from the midland hawthorn, which are both mentioned in this book, but I have listed the ash (rather than the common ash) as it is the only species of ash mentioned in the text.

Finally, only species are listed here, not groups. For example, when in the book I was talking about Australia, I mentioned platypus and kangaroos; while the platypus, a single species, is listed, the kangaroos are a group of four species, so are not listed.

The cast of trees

ʻōhiʻa lehua	*Metrosideros polymorpha*
Apple	*Malus domestica*
Apricot	*Prunus armeniaca*
Ash	*Fraxinus excelsior*
Beech	*Fagus sylvatica*
Bird cherry	*Prunus padus*
Black cherry	*Prunus serotina*
Blackthorn	*Prunus spinosa*
Coast redwood	*Sequoia sempervirens*
Common hawthorn	*Crataegus monogyna*
Cork oak	*Quercus suber*
Douglas fir	*Pseudotsuga menziesii*
Downy birch	*Betula pubescens*
Dwarf birch	*Betula nana*
Elder	*Sambucus nigra*
Evergreen oak	*Quercus ilex*
Galápagos acacia	*Vachellia rorudiana*
Ginkgo	*Ginkgo biloba*
Goat willow	*Salix caprea*
Great basin bristlecone pine	*Pinus longaeva*
Grey willow	*Salix cinerea*
Guelder rose	*Viburnum opulus*
Hazel	*Corylus avellana*
Holly	*Ilex aquifolium*
Horse chestnut	*Aesculus hippocastanum*
Hummingbird bush	*Hamelia patens*
Indian sandalwood	*Santalum album*
Juniper	*Juniperus communis*
Limber pine	*Pinus flexilis*
Maritime pine	*Pinus pinaster*
Midland hawthorn	*Crataegus laevigata*
Monkey puzzle	*Araucaria araucana*
Norway spruce	*Picea abies*
Olive	*Olea europaea*
Palo santo	*Bursera graveolens*
Peach	*Prunus persica*
Pedunculate oak	*Quercus robur*
Portuguese laurel	*Prunus lusitanica*

Rowan	*Sorbus aucuparia*
Scots pine	*Pinus sylvestris*
Serbian spruce	*Picea omorika*
Sessile oak	*Quercus petraea*
Silver birch	*Betula pendula*
Single-leaf pinyon	*Pinus monophylla*
Sitka spruce	*Picea sitchensis*
Small-leaved lime	*Tilia cordata*
Spindle	*Euonymus europaeus*
Sweet chestnut	*Castanea sativa*
Tambalacoque	*Sideroxylon grandiflorum*
Toyon	*Heteromeles arbutifolia*
Tree heather	*Erica arborea*
Umbrella thorn	*Vachellia tortilis*
Whitebark pine	*Pinus albicaulis*
Whitebeam	*Sorbus aria*
Wild cherry	*Prunus avium*
Wild tamarind	*Lysiloma latisiliquum*
Yew	*Taxus baccata*

The cast of birds

'Apapane	*Himatione sanguinea*
American robin	*Turdus migratorius*
Bald eagle	*Haliaeetus leucocephalus*
Bee-eater	*Merops apiaster*
Bee hummingbird	*Mellisuga helenae*
Black vulture	*Aegypius monachus*
Blackbird	*Turdus merula*
Blackcap	*Sylvia atricapilla*
Blue tit	*Cyanistes caeruleus*
Bonelli's eagle	*Aquila fasciata*
Buzzard	*Buteo buteo*
Cattle egret	*Bubulcus ibis*
Clark's nutcracker	*Nucifraga columbiana*
Collared dove	*Streptopelia decaocto*
Cormorant	*Phalacrocorax carbo*
Crested honeycreeper	*Palmeria dolei*
Crow	*Corvus corone*
Dodo	*Raphus cucullatus*
European robin	*Erithacus rubecula*
Fieldfare	*Turdus pilaris*
Galápagos flycatcher	*Myiarchus magnirostris*
Golden-winged sunbird	*Drepanorhynchus reichenowi*
Goshawk	*Accipiter gentilis*
Great auk	*Pinguinus impennis*
Great grey shrike	*Lanius excubitor*
Great Spotted woodpecker	*Dendrocopos major*
Great tit	*Parus major*
Green woodpecker	*Picus viridus*
Grey-headed woodpecker	*Picus canus*
Haast's eagle	*Hieraaetus moorei*
Hoatzin	*Opisthocomus hoazin*
House sparrow	*Passer domesticus*
Iberian grey shrike	*Lanius meridionalis*
Imperial woodpecker	*Campephilus imperialis*
Ivory-billed woodpecker	*Campephilus principalis*
Jackdaw	*Corvus monedula*
Jay	*Garrulus glandarius*
Kingfisher	*Alcedo atthis*

Lesser spotted woodpecker	*Dendrocopos minor*
Loggerhead shrike	*Lanius ludovicianus*
Mariana fruit dove	*Ptilinopus roseicapilla*
Mistle thrush	*Turdus viscivorus*
Mute swan	*Cygnus olor*
Northern shrike	*Lanius borealis*
Nuthatch	*Sitta europaea*
Ostrich	*Struthio camelus*
Passenger pigeon	*Ectopistes migratorius*
Ptarmigan	*Lagopus muta*
Raven	*Corvus corax*
Red-shouldered hawk	*Buteo lineatus*
Redwing	*Turdus iliacus*
Rodrigues solitaire	*Pezophaps solitaria*
Rook	*Corvus frugilegus*
Scarlet honeycreeper	*Drepanis coccinea*
Silvereye	*Zosterops lateralis*
Sociable weaver	*Philetairus socius*
Song thrush	*Turdus philomelos*
Sparrowhawk	*Accipiter nisus*
Spotted flycatcher	*Muscicapa striata*
Starling	*Sturnus vulgaris*
Streaked shearwater	*Calonectris leucomelas*
Three-toed woodpecker	*Picoides tridactylus*
Waxwing	*Bombycilla garrulus*
Wheatear	*Oenanthe oenanthe*
White stork	*Ciconia ciconia*
Woodchat shrike	*Lanius senator*
Wryneck	*Jynx torquilla*

The supporting cast

Alligator	*Alligator mississippiensis*
Aubergine	*Solanum melongena*
Avocado	*Persea americana*
Bighorn sheep	*Ovis canadensis*
Bog myrtle	*Myrica gale*
Bramble	*Rubus fruticosus*
Brown bear	*Ursus arctos*
Brown tree snake	*Boiga irregularis*
Common heather	*Calluna vulgaris*
Cucumber	*Cucumis sativus*
Eland	*Taurotragus oryx*
Giraffe	*Giraffa camelopardalis*
Green tortrix moth	*Tortrix viridana*
Haddock	*Melanogrammus aeglefinus*
Head louse	*Pediculus humanus capitis*
Honey fungus	*Armillaria mellea*
Human	*Homo sapiens*
Ivy	*Hedera helix*
Mistletoe	*Viscum album*
Mountain pine beetle	*Dendroctonus ponderosae*
Platypus	*Ornithorhynchus anatinus*
Polynesian rat	*Rattus exulans*
Reindeer	*Rangifer tarandus*
Saltwater crocodile	*Crocodylus porosus*
Spruce bark beetle	*Ips typographus*
Tapeworm	*Taenia solium*
Western gorse	*Ulex gallii*
White pine blister rust	*Cronartium ribicola*
Wild boar	*Sus scrofa*
Wild strawberry	*Fragaria vesca*
Winter moth	*Operophtera brumata*

Appendix 2 – Bird box

Naturally occurring tree holes can be scarce in gardens, but they can be easily replicated with a hole-fronted nest box. Having a nest box in your garden is a brilliant thing. Not only are you helping bird life by providing a potential breeding site, but also you are helping yourself. Nature makes you feel good. Watching wildlife is good for us; it gives us pleasure and raises our serotonin levels, it gives us a natural boost. Watching a pair of blue tits prospecting around a nest box in your garden in the New Year is a great start to the year; watching them taking nest material into it during March not only signals the imminent arrival of spring, but will bring delight, too. Watching the birds delivering beakful after beakful of caterpillars into the small hole at the front of the box during May is guaranteed to deliver joy as well. When those slightly fluffier, slightly yellower young versions of the blue tit finally fledge, the feeling you will get is quite simply brilliant. I know this because I have experienced it, I have made many a box in my time for all sorts of locations, but having one in the garden, easily viewed from the window, is such a great thing to do and experience.

The following is a quick and hopefully simple guide to making a hole-fronted nest box suitable for many species of garden bird to use. You will need a plank of 6"×1" timber measuring approximately 1.5 metres (or 5 feet) long.[124] You will also need a saw, some screws, a screwdriver, a drill with a spade bit (for its size, read on), and a twist bit, a flap of plastic or rubber, and something to attach it.

The diagram below shows the cutting layout for the plank; make the five cuts and drill your holes (read on), then you are ready to assemble the box. It is best to use screws rather than nails, especially on the lid, which you will need to take off to clean the box once the summer comes to an end. The diameter of the hole on the front depends on what species

---

124 Despite being metric in length, timber is still described in inches when it comes to width and thickness; go into any builder's merchant and ask for a piece of six by one, and they will know exactly what you are after. (The metric version is 15 cm × 2.5 cm, but if you ask for that, you are likely to get a blank look!)

of bird you wish to attract. If you don't mind, then 32 mm[125] will allow all of the tits and sparrows to use it; if you want to go for just the tit species then 28 mm will be perfect for great tit and the other smaller tits, whilst a 25 mm hole will suit blue and coal tits, and exclude the bigger species. Also, drill some small drainage holes in the base of the box. This is very important; they only have to be a standard drill bit size of a few millimetres, but they will remove any risk of the nest material getting waterlogged in very wet weather.

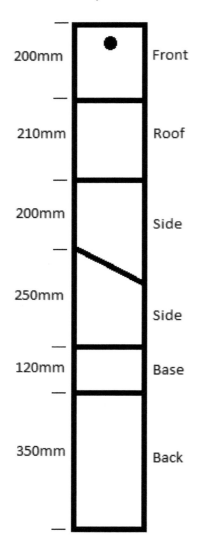

200mm — Front

210mm — Roof

200mm — Side

250mm — Side

120mm — Base

350mm — Back

Once you have cut out the pieces and drilled the holes, put the base on a level surface and place the two sides and front around it to enclose three sides of it. Screw these together, and then place it against the back of the box, roughly in the middle of that section so that you have a bit of it extending at both top and bottom (to attach the box to its support). Screw the back in place, then add the roof. This won't fit perfectly against the back because of the angle, so use the plastic or rubber to form a flap covering the gap – you can also use bathroom sealant if you have some.

The box can be fitted to any structure (fence, shed, etc) by screwing through the top and bottom extensions. But if you are attaching it to a tree, it is far better for the tree if you tie the box on, ideally using something like an old bicycle inner tube which will stretch as the tree grows. If you use string or wire, ensure that you adjust it every year after the birds have stopped nesting, to stop it cutting into the tree.

When choosing a location for your box, select somewhere that is not in full sun throughout the day and, if you can, choose a spot where you can watch it from your house, enabling you to get easy views of the box being used. Ideally the box will be at least 2.5 metres above the ground. Don't place it where a cat could access it, such as close to a top of a wall.

It is best to get your bird box up by the end of the year. Birds like blue tits might not actually nest

---

125 The type of drill bit you need for drilling the entrance holes is a spade bit; they come in a variety of sizes and are widely available from DIY stores, hardware shops, builder's merchants and of course online.

until the spring, but they will certainly be checking out potential sites in early January. So if you leave it until the spring, you may find that they have already selected a site elsewhere.

To help prolong the life of the box it is a good idea to take it down at the end of the summer and give it a bit of a clean, but don't leave it down for long, as even when it's not being used to nest in, your box is a potential resource. Many insects like the dark confines that a box has to offer, and insect-eating birds are well aware of this. I have often watched a wren disappearing into my boxes, one box after another, searching for food during the short winter days. Wrens will also use the boxes to roost in, especially during cold weather. The British Trust for Ornithology (BTO) have a record of 63 wrens roosting together in one box during a particularly nippy night, the combination of box and feathery mass tightly packed inside it keeping their temperatures up, enabling them to survive the long night. Bird boxes aren't just for nesting.

If your box isn't used straightaway, don't despair. I have had boxes that have taken a couple of years to catch the attention of prospecting birds. It's never certain that birds will use a box, but the one thing for certain is that if you don't have a bird box, then you won't get tree-hole nesting birds using your garden to breed. If you build it they will come, as someone once said …